# JESUS, HOLLYWOOD AND ME

# Jesus, Hollywood and Me

**AL KASHA AND JOEL HIRSCHHORN**

KINGSWAY PUBLICATIONS
EASTBOURNE

Produced by Bookprint Creative Services
P.O. Box 827, BN21 3YJ, England, for
KINGSWAY PUBLICATIONS LTD
Lottbridge Drove, Eastbourne, E Sussex BN23 6NT.
Printed in England by Clays Ltd, St Ives plc

**Al Kasha**

To my wife Ceil, who has always been there for me. I couldn't have done this without her.

To my daughter Dana, who has made me the proudest father in the world.

To my brother, the late Larry Kasha, who went through the wars with me and tasted the sweet fulfilment of victory. I miss him very much.

To Brian Edwards for always being in our corner.

To Martin Berger, who's been a dear friend through it all.

And

To all my talented friends from the Brill Building on Broadway, who lived the highs and lows with me:
Barry Mann, Cynthia Weil, Neil Diamond, Neil Sedaka, Howard Greenfield, Don Kirshner, Carole King, Gerry Goffin, Jack Keller, Burt Bacharach, Hal David, Jerry Lieber, Mike Stoller, Bob Dylan, Jeff Barry, Ellie Greenwich, Mort Shuman, Doc Pomus, Jackie Wilson, George David Weiss, and Aretha Franklin.

**Joel Hirschhorn**

To my wife Jennifer, for bringing me such joy with her unlimited love, friendship and creative inspiration.

# Contents

# The Morning After

Academy Award Winner: Best Original Song from the
motion picture *The Poseidon Adventure*

There's got to be a morning after,
If we can hold on through the night.
We have a chance to find the sunshine;
Let's keep on looking for the light.

Oh, can't you see the morning after?
It's waiting right outside the storm.
Why don't we cross the bridge together
And find a place that's safe and warm?

It's not too late—we should be giving.
Only with love can we climb.
It's not too late—not while we're living.
Let's put our hands out in time.

There's got to be a morning after;
We're moving closer to the shore.
I know we'll be there by tomorrow,
And we'll escape the darkness;
We won't be searching anymore.

Al Kasha
Joel Hirschhorn

# *Prologue*

## 1990

When I told my brother Larry a joke and he didn't laugh, I knew the end was near.

The Larry Kasha wit was legendary among his show business colleagues. Lauren Bacall, star of *Applause* and *Woman of the Year*, two hit Broadway musicals Larry had produced, referred to him as a 'Brooklyn Noel Coward'. He had the quickest mind of anyone I'd ever known.

And now he was staring at me, reacting literally to a funny line, unable to grasp the humour of it. The part of his brain that appreciated and created witticisms had shut down permanently.

Nothing that had happened these past months—the discovery of his illness, the endless tests, hospitalisation at Cedars Sinai in Los Angeles, watching him deteriorate physically—none of it filled me with such despair as this loss. It marked the death of my brother's personality, his core.

'I think it's time your brother got some rest,' said Harlan Kravitz, Larry's longtime doctor and the one who had originally diagnosed him as being HIV-positive.

Larry shook his head in protest.

'I've decided to stay here in the hospital room,' I told Harlan.

'Visiting hours are over.'

'No, I mean . . . stay overnight.'

Harlan shook his head. 'I'd rather you didn't.'

'I want Al with me,' Larry said. His voice was thin and

shaky, but determined.

Dr Kravitz capitulated in the face of Larry's insistence, and I spent the first of many nights in that airless, claustro-phobic room.

People get sick and die—it's a fact of life. But there are cer-tain individuals, larger-than-life personalities, who seem to possess so much power that they can vanquish death by sheer will. Larry was a personality like that. From the time we were children, he bent fate to his desire, turned obstacles into triumphs, took risks in the face of seemingly certain dis-aster. It seemed impossible that he couldn't beat AIDS too.

Beyond everything, he was my older brother. Seeing him so helpless, tossing in bed and fighting desperately to breathe, I remembered our childhood. I remembered him jumping between me and a playground bully who was threatening to beat me up. When the bully tried to hit me, Larry knocked him out cold with one punch.

He was also there, during our early childhood years, when my father went on one of his brutal, drunken ram-pages and started pounding me against the wall. Again, he pushed his way between me and my attacker and took the blows. He was the older brother I trusted and relied on.

Until he became a teenager and drifted away.

Suddenly he had new friends and a new world, and I became the outsider. Suddenly everything about me dis-pleased him: my James Dean look—black motorcycle jacket and boots, my dark sunglasses, and especially my love of rock 'n' roll. From the brother he proudly displayed, I was now the brother he sought to hide.

'Are you here?'

I heard his trembling voice in the dark, and felt his frail hand as it groped for mine.

Tears started pouring down my face, and I wiped them away with my free hand. How sad and how ironic, I thought, that after years of distance and failed reconciliations it took the horror of AIDS to make us reach out for each other.

# 1

# *Broken Bottles*

Nobody took the term 'phobia' seriously in 1945. Today psychiatrists recognise that phobias represent America's second most common mental health problem after alcoholism and refer to the 1980s as 'the age of anxiety'. But when my mother, Rose Kasha, suffered a panic attack on the subway and had to be helped from the train by concerned strangers, her symptoms were dismissed as 'nerves'. All through my childhood and beyond, she experienced sudden palpitation seizures, provoking her inevitable cry, 'I'm having a heart attack, Alfred! I'm dying—help me!'

I was petrified. I didn't want my mother to die, but even at six years old, I felt ambivalent, taken advantage of. Her attacks seemed like one more device to engulf my brother and me, one more attempt to swallow us up.

Larry felt equally frustrated. He was four years older than I was. We had little in common except fear and resentment of our parents.

We shared the same room and same small bed. I remember wishing desperately for one of my own. Larry made his feelings clear by sleeping rigidly on his side, almost tumbling off the edge. Neither of us ever slept soundly. We were too alert to danger, bracing ourselves for the moment when our father, drunk and violent, would come storming in, shouting obscenities. Usually he would yank one of us out of bed and beat us mercilessly, for reasons known only to his alcohol-fogged brain. Larry usually made the mistake of arguing back, so his beatings were more prolonged and brutal.

My mother always sobbed and begged him to stop. But when we tried to defend ourselves against his assaults she said, 'No, be nice. You'll make it worse.'

It was torture to 'be nice' to my father. He had once been an amateur wrestler in his native Poland and though only of medium height he was powerfully built, with a barrel chest and thick, granite arms. When angry and blind drunk, his powder-blue eyes would turn black and his iron knuckles sought flesh to bruise, bones to break. Larry and I were the main victims. For as long as I can remember, the big, maroon-faced man used us as regularly as a punching bag at the gym.

Until I was forty years old, I never put on a belt without dwelling on the one he wore—the one he used to hit us with. He threw chairs when someone disagreed with him, or overturned the dinner table, watching the food and drink pile messily onto the floor with sadistic satisfaction. I saw *A Streetcar Named Desire* at the age of fifteen and when I observed Marlon Brando smashing dishes, I gasped in recognition. 'Tennessee Williams must have met my father!'

My father had a habit that alienated sons and strangers alike, of shaking your hand and crushing it until the pain was unbearable. After arguments, he would say to me in a conciliatory tone, 'Let's make up. Shake,' and I would extend my hand as he watched. His hand was powerfully developed from opening and closing the scissors he used daily as a barber, and when they folded around my fingers, I bit my tongue, struggling to smother the cries roaring in my throat. He kept staring, measuring me, waiting for me to break.

'Be nice,' my mother continued to say, so I suppressed my natural instinct for self-defence. I absorbed her message, 'peace at any price', burying my rage while it ate away at me, resulting in headaches and excruciating stomach pains.

I once asked my Aunt Tessie, my father's sister, why he behaved so viciously. 'He doesn't mean it, Alfred,' she told me. 'His father beat him up; it's the only way he knows.' But at six years old, I couldn't forgive him.

I also couldn't know that my father was a bitterly frustrated man, married to a woman who had only contempt for him. Often he yelled at her, 'Always the sons, always the sons. Never me, always the sons.' He pulled me into a corner when I was eight and mumbled, 'Look at your mother. *Look* at her!' For a second I saw her through his eyes—short, plump, with small brown eyes and thick lips. 'Your mother doesn't know how to please a man. Do you understand what I'm saying?' I didn't understand exactly, but I knew it was something I didn't want to hear. I was too young to grasp the genuine agony behind the confession. I saw that agony more clearly another time when I found him sobbing in the kitchen. He cried for days. My mother explained, 'A letter came from his nephew in Warsaw. . . . His father and two brothers were shot and killed by the Nazis.'

She was sympathetic for once. But most of the time she grieved about her marriage to 'that animal', saying she was scared to death of him, that the only thing in life of any importance was her two boys. 'You and Larry—you're all I have,' was her favourite theme.

The message was obvious: 'It's up to you and Larry to rescue me.'

I knew my mother had once loved a man. She often spoke of a Mr Klinger, the pharmacist; and her features softened when she mentioned him. My mother loved to sing around the flat. Her favourite song was 'You'll Never Know Just How Much I Love You', and I sensed she was singing that song especially for him.

'He used to bring me flowers every time he came to the house,' she said. 'He had no money, but he always found enough for a bouquet. He wanted to marry me, you know, but I was crazy. I married your father.' And then her tears would flow. 'I married your father because he was so handsome and such a good dancer. What do you know at sixteen, Alfred? You never think a man has to make a living.'

I was ten years old when my mother and I were stopped on Avenue L by a short, balding gentleman with a moustache.

'Rose,' he said.

My mother blushed like a schoolgirl. 'Hello, Harvey. Harvey Klinger, this is my son, Alfred.'

Harvey bowed his shiny head, then smiled. 'You look pretty, Rose.' In my mind, I suddenly heard my mother's voice singing 'You'll Never Know'.

When they shook hands and said goodbye, my mother was, for the only time I knew her, beautiful.

The most embarrassing aspect of our flat, to me, was its location over a shop my parents jointly owned. They ran a business, unimaginatively titled 'Rose and Irving's', a combination barber shop and beauty parlour. My mother's iron determination and business acumen kept the business going during the depression years. It certainly wasn't her ability as a manicurist or beautician; her idea of dyeing hair was to make everything as garishly blonde or black as possible. My father was more talented as a barber, with everybody's head but mine. He insisted on cutting off all my hair, making me look perilously close to a monk or a Hare Krishna follower. I vowed I would let my hair grow long, like Samson, when I was old enough.

His mood swings also created crises. Once he got into an argument with a customer and chased him into the street with a pair of scissors, slashing the customer's arm and drawing blood. The customer pressed charges, but they were later dropped.

My father's other problem was even more worrying: his bigotry. It was always simmering beneath the surface. He served blacks reluctantly, occasionally refusing to cut their hair, and his lifelong hatred of the *goyim* (Gentiles), particularly Catholics, triggered off rudeness when one of the 'enemy camp' sat in his chair. As a child in Poland, my father had been beaten viciously by anti-Semites, and the mental wounds remained fresh and raw throughout his life.

My mother and I would sit at the cash register after the disturbances died down and she would confide: 'He beat me today.' Or, 'He embarrassed me in front of a customer.'

Sometimes she would say, 'I wish I could leave him. But what then? Tell me. There's no money. . . and what about the shop? If I didn't take care of it, it would fall apart. You know your father—he can't take care of anything.'

'Don't worry, Mum,' I assured her, with the fervent logic of a child. 'Someday I'll buy you a mink coat and you'll have a big car and a house.'

'I'm depending on you, darling,' she would say, hugging the breath out of me. 'You're the way out, you and your brother. You're the way out.'

My role as rescuer was established then, and every time my father inflicted physical or emotional wounds on my mother, she would remind me, 'You're the way out. Remember.'

To raise her spirits I wrote little poems for her, and she saved them. One said:

Mum, you're the greatest,
more than the rest.
And someday, Mum, you'll have the best.

It was easier, even then, to express myself in rhyme or

through melodies than to spell out my feelings.

With each poem, Mum would thank me and emphasise, 'I'll leave him when you and Larry make enough money.' I thought, *If I do enough, achieve enough, make her dreams come true, she'll have the courage to walk out.* Most kids from troubled homes wanted their parents to patch things up and stay together. I dreamed of the day my parents would get divorced.

*If my mother left him, she'd be safe. We'd all be safe.*

Part of me hated the barber shop; hated the smell of shampoo and shaving cream. I had a recurring nightmare of hair down my back, sticking to my skin, making me itch. In the dream, I'd throw myself into scalding hot showers, trying to wash the hair from my skin, but it clung, each follicle a blood-sucking insect.

Life wasn't much better when I was awake. Larry and I had to wash the floors, and my father stood over us, screaming, 'You left out a spot there. What's the matter with you dummies? Use a little muscle!' Larry was an excellent student at Madison High, and my teachers constantly told my parents how much talent I had in music, but my father measured us by our ability to keep the floors clean. Once, in anger, he stepped on my right hand and broke a finger, because we had accidentally neglected a corner.

The shop did have a positive aspect, however. Since my parents were hopeless role models, it offered healthier personalities to emulate. I was an attentive listener and a natural mimic and I memorised everything about the parade of customers I met, soaking in their mannerisms, their modes of dress, their speech patterns. They became a huge substitute family. Some were famous—Arthur Miller came to have his hair cut; so did Rocky Graziano. I entertained by singing and doing impersonations of Al Jolson (whom I loved after seeing *The Jolson Story*) and Frank Sinatra. The father of opera star Leonard Warren said, 'You could sing in the opera, like my boy.' I treasured that compliment, even though my father howled with laughter afterwards, calling Mr Warren 'stupid' for saying it.

At nine and ten I was chubby and red-cheeked—the kind of child adults wanted to pinch—and I worked at being lovable. I needed unqualified approval to survive. I don't remember my father ever uttering a word of praise, and my mother viewed my achievements as accomplishments of her own. 'You came out of my body,' she was fond of saying, patting a protruding stomach. 'You're like me; you're talented like I am.'

Or she would pit me against my brother, stirring up a sibling rivalry that made closeness impossible.

'Be like your brother Larry. . . he gets such good marks.'

'Be like your brother Alfred. . . he is such a good singer.'

'Be like your brother Larry. . . he's such a wonderful dancer.'

'Be like your brother Alfred. . . he's so good at sport.'

Larry's being forced to assume full responsibility for me during the day didn't help. When it counted he was in my corner, protecting me from bullies when they started fights. But he resented taking me to school and picking me up. He had to help me with my homework—a chore he approached reluctantly. When he met his friends, my mother automatically insisted, 'Take Alfred along.'

Among his peers, I saw my brother blossom. He was witty, a real comedian, the life and soul of the party. Sadly, this sense of fun was stamped out at home.

Both Larry and I dreamed of a show business career one day. He would dance like Gene Kelly and I would sing like Frank Sinatra (similar ambitions that would have created competition in the most peaceful of families).

We also dreamed of escaping our tiny, cockroach-infested flat, with its mud-brown walls and clanging radiator. Larry was particularly upset by the combined smell of hair dye and alcohol—an aroma that choked healthy air out of the premises.

What upset Larry most, though, was having to share his clothes with me. We were both heavy as children, so his hand-me-downs were a comfortable fit.

Larry was incredibly tidy and meticulous—everything neatly hung and arranged in his wardrobe—and he accused me of dirtying his shirts and trousers when I played ball.

I realised the full extent of his animosity when he turned thirteen and lost nearly two stone in weight.

'These trousers are too small for me,' I said, when my mother asked me to try on a pair of Larry's grey tweed trousers.

Larry was sitting at the kitchen table doing his maths homework. He looked up through brown-rimmed glasses, eyes blazing.

'I'm gonna be so skinny,' he said, 'that you'll *never* be able to wear my clothes again.'

I never felt close to him again—at least not until we were grown up and able to sort out the destructive things our parents had done to us. The bed we shared seemed smaller than ever now, and it was vitally important to maintain a distance. Never to touch again, even accidentally.

Lying on my back at night, staring at the cracks in the ceiling, I talked to God a lot. I always dimly understood that God was dependable; a force that would never fail me the way people did.

'Dear God,' I remember whispering, 'make my daddy stop drinking.' I waited for an answer, as the underground rattled and shook our building, and buses raced past my street corner. I prayed with more urgency when I over-heard my father smashing a bottle of vodka against the mirror in his bedroom. I thought of all the bottles I had hidden or poured away, all the bottles my mother had diluted with water.

'Dear God,' went another prayer, 'don't let Daddy hurt

Mum.' But that prayer went unanswered too. My mother's face was often black and blue in the morning; her face cut by the jagged edges of broken bottles, deformed by fists, lamps, any handy object that could wreak damage.

Sometimes I pictured these scenes during the day, when I was away from home and supposedly safe: during a class, in the changing rooms after gym, having lunch. And the panic would build up in me, accompanied by sweaty palms and dizziness. Once I ran out of a hot, crowded classroom. Another time a friend crept up behind me in the corridor and covered my eyes. He meant it as a joke, but I felt so startled and confined by those hands that I leaped at him, punching him and knocking him down. A teacher had to wrench us apart. I remember the stunned look on my friend's freckled face. My violence shocked him because I had always been so mild-mannered.

At times like those, the room would shake, and I had a sense that the ground would open up underneath me and drag me millions of feet into a black void.

Still, I was stubborn. I felt there was a reason for it all; that God would never abandon me. If I just held on, all this misery and madness would somehow make sense.

# 2

# *The Way Out*

Much as I despised Brooklyn, I loved the fact that our flat was across the road from Warner Brothers' Vitagraph Studios. In the late 1930s and 1940s, they were making two-reelers, and my mother managed to get Larry in a few of them as an extra. I even appeared in one.

My parents were frequently asked to cut an actor's hair or do his nails, so I had an ideal excuse to hang around. I remember my father grumbling that Jack Haley (the Tin Man in *The Wizard of Oz*) had no beard, so shaving him was a waste of time. My mother nursed a grudge against lyricist Sammy Cahn because he didn't give her a tip after she found the plane ticket he had lost. Fatty Arbuckle was a shining star who worked there before the rape scandal that destroyed his career.

My child's eye blinked away the imperfections. These were all glamorous, successful beings, and one day I would be one of them—singing, acting, doing my impressions on film.

'Show business is for little girls, not men,' my father bellowed. 'You're not a little girl, are you?'

'No.'

'Hey, you're not mad, are you?'

'I'm not mad.'

'Sure you are. OK, I'm sorry. Let's make up. Shake!' He extended his hand and squashed my knuckles until pain shot through my fingers and up my arm.

My father objected strongly to any creative pursuits, but my mother gave us dancing and singing lessons anyway. She learned where auditions were from talk around the Vitagraph Studios. Each casting call made my father more angry; he wanted at least one of his sons to become a doctor because his older brother, whom he idolised, had a flourishing medical practice. He screamed, 'Shut up!' when my mother sang. She usually continued with 'You'll Never Know', raising her voice louder in defiance. He would snarl, 'You can't *sing*, Rose. You have a lousy voice. You can't sing, and your son can't sing either. I don't want that noise around here!'

'You'll never know just how much I care. . . .'

Those lyrics wounded him, because he knew they weren't for him. Larry and I watched the same scene unfold daily: her singing, his deafening wrath, her refusal to stop, provoking a slap if she was lucky or a punch if she wasn't.

'I won't stop,' she would sob. 'I'll sing around here and so will my sons. You animal. You can't stop me!'

Terrified as she was of his violence, my mother, who bent on nearly every issue, wouldn't surrender the few moments of happiness she experienced when singing. Singing was the only way of asserting her dream, letting him know her sons would succeed in show business. Through singing, she made it clear that she, Larry and I would spring from the ghetto cage one day, leaving him behind.

In my mother's fantasy, she was the pampered focus of her sons' lives, revelling in their triumphs, decked out in furs and jewels on Broadway opening nights. We were her escape route and no girl was good enough for us. Even at nine or ten they were competition. 'Boys should be with boys and girls with girls,' was one of her familiar statements. Most of the Jewish mothers I knew felt that way about their sons, but my mother's reactions were extreme.

She warned us, 'Don't let a woman trap you'—advice I could have benefited from in the years to follow. Still, whether consciously aware of it or not, her attitude was disturbingly seductive. She walked around the flat without a blouse, in her bra and sometimes without it. My mother was a heavy woman with enormous breasts, and the sight of her nudity made me uncomfortable.

Singing in the temple provided a welcome refuge from family pressure. I was eagerly encouraged by a cantor named Alvin Cooper. Cantor Cooper had thick, black, wavy hair and grimly downturned eyebrows; but I knew he admired my voice. I sang for him with all the passion my ten-year-old vocal cords could muster.

'God is applauding you,' he said once, and I felt excited and proud. 'Someday you'll be a cantor. Just promise me one thing, Alfred. Always sing Yiddish music. Don't go into the opera like Jan Peerce and Richard Tucker.' Both these great singers had been cantors before making their mark on the opera world. 'It would be a *shonda*, Alfred, a shame,' he concluded.

My maternal grandfather also thought of me as a future cantor. I allowed both men to believe I would seriously consider it. Religion was important to me during that period. I loved Hebrew school and loved attending synagogue on the holidays.

Religion, to me, was a promise. To my Russian grandfather it was life itself. He was an imposing figure, even at 5'6", with a reddish goatee, moustache and stringy hair. He usually wore a hat with a yarmulke beneath it.

My grandmother was quieter and sweeter; she rarely said a word, and when she did it was only in Yiddish. She looked at her husband with mute adoration while he conducted four-hour Passover seders that occasionally taxed my youthful patience.

But football and girls eventually claimed all my attention and Cantor Cooper, recognising my change of attitude, transferred his affections to another boy at the synagogue.

My show business career really began in 1945 when I was seven years old. After auditioning for *Annie Get Your Gun*, producers Rodgers and Hammerstein chose me to play Ethel Merman's baby brother, Jake, replacing Warren Berlinger.

I recall Mr Rodgers as a cool, formidable person, but Mr Hammerstein was warm and encouraging. I lived for the times he smiled in my direction. I was always choosing fantasy fathers to replace my own, and he fit the bill perfectly—someone I could respect, someone who would stand behind me and my aspirations. I worked up enough courage to say, 'Hi, Mr Hammerstein,' when he was backstage and he waved back. Once he even patted me firmly on the head.

When the time came for *Annie Get Your Gun* to tour, I was asked to stay with it, but my mother couldn't leave Rose and Irving's to travel with me. I begged her to change her mind; I cried. I got down on my knees, like Al Jolson doing 'Mammy'. (Even at seven, I had a keen theatrical sense.) Nothing worked. I was a modern Dickensian victim, except that my personal prison was a barber shop, not a bottle factory.

My mother continued to do what she could, in addition to slaving away at the shop. She wrote to Warner Brothers in Hollywood on 2nd December 1946, asking them to consider me for feature films. Their response was a standard letter: not interested at this time. I still have the letter, and I have to admit it gave me satisfaction in 1975 to win a Best Song Oscar for a Warner Brothers picture, *The Towering Inferno*.

My creative energies focused on school. I wrote shows, organised them, cast them and gave myself starring parts. Sometimes my casting ideas backfired, particularly when I persuaded my teacher to give me the romantic lead in *The Student Prince*. I was at my heaviest and the audience giggled when I walked on stage.

I soon realised that the best route to gain attention was becoming class clown. I answered teachers with wisecracks and made faces behind their backs. 'Did you hear the one about. . .' became my standard phrase.

There was nothing I didn't plan to be at one time or another, as long as it meant maintaining a grip on the limelight: actor, singer, comic, impressionist, writer, producer, director. 'I want to please; notice me' were the signals I sent out, and people responded. Most people who are in show business have this need for attention—even the ones who express a passion for privacy. Adulthood and increasing security act as tempering influences, but the childlike 'Love me, love me' is never totally silenced.

I was anything but silent in those years. But my high-pressure, workaholic drive was palatable because I spoke softly. I had a courteous, gentle manner because I loathed my father's loudness.

At eleven I starred in the school variety show, playing Curly in *Oklahoma*. The audience cheered, but my father ruined everything by coming to the performance drunk, and roaring, 'Where's my Alfred?' All heads in the auditorium spun around. Later, at home, I couldn't help saying, 'Daddy, why did you have to talk?'

His response was to give me the worst beating I'd ever received. He grabbed me by both shoulders and threw me against a cupboard door. He hammered those huge fists against my ribs.

'Is that the way you talk to your father?' he shouted, as I fought to struggle free.

'Mum!' I screamed. 'Make him stop!'

'Irving, leave him alone.'

'Shut up, Rose,' he warned, raising his fist menacingly. She shrank back.

'That's enough,' she said, compromising between her instinct for motherhood and her own personal terror.

He clubbed me on the arms, elbows, shoulders.

'That'll teach you, big shot.'

Totally out of control, he picked up a half-empty brandy bottle and smashed it over my head. I felt blood spurting from my scalp.

Then he yanked open the bedroom cupboard and shoved me inside, slamming the door.

'How does that feel, big shot?' he shouted, as I pounded wildly on the door. Blood dripped down my cheeks, onto my lips. I swallowed it.

'Please, Daddy, let me out!'

'Big shot.'

I can still smell the shoe leather and the suffocating moth-balls in that cupboard; still feel the suits and shirts dangling like dead bodies.

'Daddy, please! I can't breathe!'

He cackled drunkenly, ignoring my pleas. 'I'll be good,' I swore, not comprehending what good was; willing to promise anything to wrench free of the dark cell he had forced me into.

'I'll be good, I'll be good.'

'How do you like it now, big shot?'

Then I overheard scuffling. I heard my mother pleading, as usual, and Larry's outraged voice. He had just returned from acting in a local play. My father's brute force had blocked Larry from opening the door, but in the next fifteen minutes there were other voices, footsteps.

The door shot open and I fell out, shaking and sobbing helplessly. I found myself in the comforting arms of a policeman.

It was the first time the police had been summoned to break up one of our family quarrels. They wanted to lock my father up, but my mother begged them to give him another chance.

'He's still your father,' she explained, after the officers had left and he was helped into bed.

'He's crazy,' Larry shouted. 'A stupid, crazy animal.'

'He's your father,' she repeated. 'You don't want him put in jail like some criminal, do you?'

'Yes,' Larry screamed. 'Before he kills you. . . or us. Mum, look. . . look at your son. Look at his face. Look at the blood. *Look*!'

'Your father's not always like that. If he didn't drink so much. . . .'

'But he does.'

'Think of the disgrace if your father goes to jail. Think of what the neighbours will say.'

'Who cares about the neighbours?'

'Darling, don't yell. My blood pressure.'

Larry quietened down.

'It's not like he goes to bars.'

'No,' said Larry. 'It's OK because he gets smashed at home.'

'He doesn't go to bars,' she repeated. 'And besides, what about the business if he goes to jail? Will people come if they know Irving Kasha's in jail?' She paused. 'It's not like he's some common drinker, some *shicka* off the street.'

She didn't conclude with her usual words, but Larry and I heard them just the same.

'Be nice.'

# 3
# *Bingeing*

I was grateful to Larry for saving me. I took his intervention as a sign of caring. He did care—I know that now—
but he couldn't allow anyone, even me, to sidetrack him
emotionally. He felt our environment was evil and would
drag him down unless he pulled free of it altogether.

He was never unkind, only quiet. By the time I had my
bar mitzvah we barely spoke, and the circumstances were
such a disappointment that I finally cut myself off from
him emotionally as well.

Four years earlier, my parents had hired a hall for a
reception following Larry's bar mitzvah service. Now, in
January of 1950, with money a greater problem than ever,
they held my reception in our flat. I was bitterly resentful
and jealous. A bar mitzvah reception above a shop! I
deserved better than that. I had thrown myself into my
Hebrew studies with enthusiasm. I had made my mother
proud by singing in the temple and at parties and weddings.

Nothing lifted my spirits—not even the numerous presents and cheques my relatives handed me. I sang 'Thou
Swell', accompanied by a piano player my parents had
hired. Larry had had a three-piece band.

I was embarrassed by my haircut too—my father had
cut it so short I looked prematurely bald. I remember the
haircut vividly. When I protested, my father hissed in my
ear, 'Shut up. . . or I'll throw you in the cupboard.'

Hours later I was still brooding over the threat, remembering the sensation of that narrow, airless cupboard, when a chance remark by my Aunt Helen distracted me. I was eating a chopped liver sandwich when I overheard Aunt Helen, my one skinny relative, comment loudly to my mother, 'Rose, what are you feeding Alfred? He's so fat!'

'He looks fine,' my mother said. I thought of the Boy Scout hike I had participated in a year ago. All my friends' mothers had packed sausages; mine had packed three lamb chops with careful cooking instructions. Her idea of roughing it in the woods meant a feast. God forbid her son should starve.

The seams in my suit were bursting—another hand-me-down from Larry. I heard my mother say, 'He's a growing boy.' The trouble was, I was growing in the wrong direction. What was charmingly chubby on a six-year-old looked merely gross on a teenager. I knew it and felt desperately ashamed, but I couldn't stop eating.

Even that day, stung by my aunt's assessment, I hovered around the buffet table, stuffing down turkey, bagels, potato salad, rolls and pastries. In fact, the remark only doubled my appetite. The sense of deprivation I felt could only be satisfied with food.

I had to have it.

Family mealtimes were never less than a nightmare for me. I ate out of a nervous compulsion to do something with my hands. After jamming mountainous portions of food down my throat, I was inevitably sick afterwards. Cramps were a daily occurrence.

To savour eating without the accompaniment of family hysterics, I would rush home from school and sneak in a separate pre-dinner meal of my own. I didn't want to risk provoking my parents, so I ate twice. By thirteen, after years of gobbling down four meals a day, I weighed 15½ st. My mother would say, as mothers of the 1940s always did, 'Think of the poor, starving children in Europe.' My appetite was so large by then that I ate not only for Europe, but for Africa, India and the Far East as well.

'Hey, here comes Kareshape,' my friend Barry was fond of saying. The nickname came from a Dick Tracy character named Pearshape, who had bulging, oversized hips. The description fit only too well. Barry was tall and lean, with curly brown hair and the kind of broad shoulders and trim waist that girls favoured. From my point of view, he had everything—a loving father, the kind I wished I had, and a mother who worshipped him and hung on his every word. He was a born actor, a born artist, a born athlete. Nature had showered him with gifts, but I was too in awe of them to be jealous.

At school all the girls fell in love with Barry. He was captain of the cheerleaders. He was the first of my friends to 'go all the way'. And he collected 'A's for every exam without studying.

At the time, I wondered why someone like Barry would lower himself to befriend roly-poly me. He laughed at my frenzied activity. I was always organising something—the Sing Show (conceived by my brother four years earlier), the Junior Show, the School Dance. I belonged to the chorus. And most crucially—because I believe it maintained my sanity—I played football.

I wasn't a great football player like Barry. I didn't have his height or his muscle. But I had one quality that made me valuable to the team—I wanted to win. The same intensity and sublimated anger that made me strive for recognition as an entertainer served me well on the football field. I was hostile, violent—as violent as my father. Every tackle was charged with a fury I couldn't unleash at home.

Off the field I continued to be gentle; I spoke in a whisper. No one could define me, though, because I kept trying new identities. No sooner would someone say, 'He's so sweet and quiet,' than I would burst into a wild Red Skelton or Milton Berle routine. I had a rubber face, a Jerry

Lewis face, puffing up my lips, crossing my eyes. Then the class clown would dissolve, and I'd take on the role of muted, silent guru, listening to people's problems with the patience of an analyst. A lifetime of concentrating on my mother's various grievances had trained me to be a willing ear. I 'rescued' strangers, the way I kept trying to rescue my mother.

I wavered schizophrenically between adult and infant, slipping into whatever emotional costume would work in a given situation.

'Who are you, Kareshape?' Barry once asked me. I certainly couldn't have told him.

I fell in love for the first time at sixteen. The object: a dark, tiny girl named Marlene, with two oversized attributes—singing voice and bust. Both of them mesmerised me, particularly the voice. Marlene wanted to star on Broadway someday, and we shared our dreams of future glory. Our mutual fantasising was so important to her that she pulled away during lunch from her group of girlfriends, a brave and independent act for a 1950s high school junior.

She gave me hope when she said, 'You know, Al, if you went on a diet, you could be very attractive.' I raced home that day with new resolve; I would starve off the ungainly pounds. I'd cut out my secret meal. If I was slim and handsome, maybe Marlene would go steady with me through high school, even college. And maybe then we'd write shows together, or co-star in a Broadway musical. Even at sixteen I had big dreams, setting my sights on the seemingly impossible.

The diet lasted two days. One clash with my father, one nagging word from my mother and I scrambled to the freezer to stuff satisfaction into myself. Satisfaction usually took the form of ice cream; I was addicted to it, particularly chocolate.

'I lost three pounds,' I lied to Marlene during a chorus rehearsal.

'Great. I knew you could do it.'

I kept planning to start the diet again. . . planning to have one sandwich for lunch instead of three, planning to cut out my ice cream after school.

Marlene and I sneaked into the music room whenever it was empty and worked out duets, most of them from shows like *Carousel* and *The King and I*. Sometimes we practised at her house, either to Marlene's piano backing or to records. I never brought her to my flat. My mother would have found reasons to rip Marlene apart, and I didn't think I could stand that.

'Barry is awfully nice,' Marlene commented off-hand-edly one afternoon.

'He's terrific,' I agreed. 'Not only is he the best student and the best athlete, it comes easily to him.'

'I guess he's just lucky. I bet he'll be the first Jewish pres-ident.'

A few weeks later I saw Marlene and Barry huddling together in the hall. They noticed me coming and jumped apart. Barry said hello with false heartiness, and Marlene asked me—at this tactically humiliating time—how my diet was progressing.

'I lost another five pounds.' Actually I had gained. My trousers were slicing me around the waist and I found it murderously hard to tuck my shirts in.

Barry grabbed me at football practice and asked if I minded his taking Marlene out. 'Really, Kareshape, if there's anything between you two, I'll step aside,' he vol-unteered magnanimously.

*Stop calling me 'Kareshape'.*

'No, we're just friends,' I assured him. I couldn't believe the tears that were flooding my eyes. 'Have to run.'

I had never known such pain, not even when my father was hitting me.

'The hell with you, Barry,' I muttered to myself in the boy's toilets after my crying had subsided. 'Someday *I'll* be the first Jewish president.'

Fat chance. Especially if Barry was my competitor.

Life has given me a few swift kicks, but sometimes it has delivered exciting, unexpected possibilities through the back door. That year I was asked to run for school president. The kids who nominated me were the outsiders—the 'brains', the non-athletes, the ones with enough individuality to reject clubs and cliques, or were too old to be accepted by them. I was one of these. Because I sang and clowned about I had a high profile, but I never quite belonged.

The idea was scary but appealing. Still, I wasn't sure until Barry informed me he was also planning to try for the honour.

'May the best man win,' I said, grinning, surprising myself. I think he expected old Kareshape automatically to drop out and leave the arena clear. I still remember the funny tightening of his eyes, even though he pretended to smile.

Another thought intimidated me—the knowledge that my brother had been vice-president of Madison four years earlier. I dreaded losing, of failing to meet Larry's standard.

'I won't think that way,' I decided. 'I'll plunge full steam ahead and battle Barry for every vote.' From that minute on I was obsessed with the contest. I asked my supporters to write out 'Kasha for President' pamphlets, and I devised a slogan (SOS—Save Our School), which seemed suitably urgent. I had banners made and gave speeches in the playground, the gym or in front of the water fountain. Inspiring names like Lincoln, Washington and Roosevelt dominated my thoughts.

I never slept. By sixteen I was a fully-fledged insomniac. Usually I crept into the kitchen and continued snacking. When I did briefly sink into sleep, images of myself trapped in a wardrobe woke me up again. I became alert to

the danger of that dream, an emotion that phobic special-
ists of the 1980s referred to as 'anticipatory anxiety'. Sleep
represented the terror of confinement; awake I could protect myself.

But I couldn't protect myself against Marlene's lack of
belief in me. She caught up with me after chorus one day
and said, 'Don't feel bad if you lose, Al.'

'I'm not losing,' I swore. Her attitude made me push
harder.

Barry hardly campaigned. His relaxed attitude infuriated me. He was still friendly, in a patronising way,
although his wisecracks ('Put on a few, didn't you?') were
amiably wounding. He indicated that it was bad form to
try so hard; vulgar to chase after approval.

Our principal announced the results on the football field.
It was a drizzling, windy November day, and I had a cold.

'Treasurer. . . Barry Freed. Vice President. . . Richard
"Tiny" Levine. . .'

I was beaten. All the officers belonged to Barry's contin-
gent.

'President. . .' A momentary hesitation; the principal
was clearly startled. 'Alfred Jerome Kasha.'

The field erupted into applause. I was so shocked and
overjoyed that I didn't even mind the use of my hated
middle name.

'Yeah, Big Al!' someone shouted. At first I winced,
thinking that big meant 'fat', but seconds later I recognised
it as a compliment, an expression of admiration.

Miracles were possible!

'Thank you, God,' I said under my breath.

I thought of Larry; his kid brother had carried the Kasha
banner forward. And my parents—they'd have to admit
their son had pulled off a remarkable feat.

Barry wandered unsteadily over to shake my hand. He
looked bewildered, a damp and defeated Golden Boy who
had aged before my eyes.

'Hey, you did it, Kare—' He stopped. 'Kasha.' His taut lips appeared to be framing the question '*Why?*'.

I understood then that rewards—a class presidency, any kind of success—only come about by relentless effort, sheer tenacity and struggle. Natural ability is just the first step.

I was transformed, for a few hours, into a Golden Boy myself. It was a short victory. Marlene, after bestowing a congratulatory kiss on my cheek, walked off with Barry. I watched them disappear, arm in arm, leaving me alone on the now-empty football field.

The royal rug of the presidency was pulled out from under me at the end of my junior year. In July, President Kasha became a busboy at the Karmel Hotel for the summer. Located in the Catskill Mountains, this Borscht Belt prison was owned by my Uncle Perry, my mother's youngest brother. Understaffed by any standard, the Karmel employed five busboys to service 300 people. The pay amounted to slightly less than slave labour. Uncle Perry used to whip me into line by saying, 'Working hard builds character.'

I began the depressing experience of building character every morning at 6.30. The five busboys shared one bunk. Standing under the shower was like being rained on by cubes of falling ice. From there the day slid downhill. My first responsibility was to cut up grapefruits; there was a minimum of 200 to handle daily and I was less than graceful about it. My fingers would slip from the centre of the grapefruit and I always wondered what the guests' comments would be if they knew they were eating grapefruit covered all over by Al Kasha's finger.

Larry worked at the Karmel too. He held a higher position—waiter—and also staged a couple of amateur shows. He still enjoyed acting, but his directing and producing ambitions had begun to flower. The brilliance that later earned him a Tony was already in evidence.

My brother was always outgoing, but now he became flamboyantly theatrical. He lost weight and wore skin-tight trousers. All his spare time was spent at the gym, lifting weights, running around the track, doing more push-ups than any tyrannical army sergeant would have demanded.

Sometimes I caught him in front of a mirror, examining himself with a medical attention to detail. The progress of every developing muscle was scrupulously examined; he studied his legs, his thighs, his stomach (which was never flat enough to satisfy him), the width of his neck.

When he wasn't in the gym working on his body, Larry worked on his dancing. He would watch Fred Astaire in *Top Hat*, or Gene Kelly in *An American in Paris* and imitate their steps. To my biased brotherly eye, he was even better than the masters he imitated.

I was totally the opposite. I felt clumsy on the dance floor. It didn't help that I kept adding on pounds at the same rapid rate Larry lost them.

Finally I summoned up the nerve to ask my brother to help me—to teach me how to dance—so I could impress Marlene. At first he refused, but then, seeing my obvious disappointment, he agreed to give me a lesson. He put on Tito Puente's famous mambo, 'Oye Como Va'. 'But you've got to concentrate,' he said severely, making me freeze even more. Larry had a critical, dissatisfied attitude that always made me feel I could never measure up to his stan-dards. Still, I was so determined to dance smoothly that I ignored the imperious tone of voice.

'Here,' he said, taking my hands. 'I'll lead. . . now watch carefully to see what I'm doing.'

He twirled me around the gym floor. Others were start-ing to stare, and I sensed they were laughing at me.

'You're not concentrating,' Larry snapped impatiently.

He was right; the situation suddenly felt horribly awk-

ward and wrong. Something about Larry's movements—
the tilt of his head, the Ginger Rogers-type angle of his
shoulders—gave me my first awareness that he was gay.

Or at least *acting* gay. I wasn't ready to admit he might
actually be gay, but our dancing together forced me to
recognise more than I wanted to.

'I'm just no good,' I said, pulling away.

Larry didn't argue; he was relieved that our lesson was
at an end. Neither of us ever tried to repeat the experiment.

Poor dancer that I was, I was still instructed to dance
with the guests. They were usually older women, and it
was unspoken but understood that they needed sexual
attention during the week while their husbands worked in
the hot city.

Many of the Karmel employees were happy to oblige. I
felt the same hammering lust they did, but I wanted something more; romance, love, a feeling of exclusivity. I still
pined after Marlene. I even wrote her a letter, but she never
answered. The ultimate heartbreak occurred when her
parents came up to spend three weeks at the Karmel and
she didn't join them. 'Marlene was supposed to come,' her
mother rattled on thoughtlessly, 'but she didn't want to
leave Barry. You know Barry, don't you Al?'

'Yes, I know Barry.'

Rescue finally arrived in the form of a girl named Sarah,
the baker's daughter. Sarah had heavy thighs and arms,
but her generous breasts always appeared to be tipped in
my direction and she had dazzling white teeth against a
dark complexion. We blundered through sex and all I
could think of was, 'Well, I did it.' Another milestone
reached and not very exciting.

Still, women were willing to sleep with me even if I was
chubby. Sarah and I had eating in common of course (we
gorged ourselves at every opportunity) and she shared my
love of theatre. On nights off we would roam from hotel to
hotel, watching their shows and comparing them to what

Larry was doing for the Karmel. I saw more bad musicians, boring comedians, tone-deaf singers and wooden actors than I would have thought possible. I caught old-timers like Harry Richmond. Occasionally I was fortunate enough to catch great comedians like Red Buttons and Dick Van Dyke.

Sarah and I lasted four weeks into the summer. Love, or my frantic efforts to see it that way, ended when I passed a mirror in the lobby. Sarah and I were both in bathing suits and we looked like twins: walking blobs of flesh holding hands. My curly hair and boyish grin looked as though they were welded to the body of a middle-aged man. Sarah's posture was bent, making her seem ten years older than her actual age, fifteen.

In typical extreme fashion (I never did anything by halves) I gave up eating. Grapefruit and coffee sustained me through the gruelling hours, but I was determined to pass that lobby mirror on Labor Day and see a human being of normal proportions. Sarah refused to diet. 'I only need to lose five pounds,' she protested. I knew our staying together would kill my discipline and tempt me into old patterns.

Reluctantly I said goodbye to her.

That summer I also met a brash, energetic pianist named Jack Keller. Jack was so hyperactive he made me look catatonic; his mouth was always moving, his feet and hands competed for a nervous tic award. He was a dreamer, like me, and we decided to work together when the summer ended. Jack would be my accompanist and we'd 'make some decent bread' (Jack's words) doing weddings and dances until he got on his feet as a songwriter.

I didn't realise it then, but Jack was one of a group of Brooklyn natives destined to make rock 'n' roll history in the late 1950s and early 1960s. All of them attended Madison or Lincoln High and all lived within twenty blocks of each other. They included Neil Sedaka, his partner Howie

Greenfield, Barry Mann ('You Lost That Lovin' Feelin'), Mort Schuman ('Save the Last Dance for Me' and 'Teenager in Love'), Neil Diamond and Carole King. In 1970, a trade paper claimed that the combination of these Brooklyn-born composers (including me) accounted for the sale of over 700 million records.

I still couldn't identify completely with Jack's passion for writing. Writing was the work of anonymous contributors, and I was no shadow. I wanted to be seen and applauded, because applause was proof I existed. Direct acknowledgement and praise were necessities since I received neither at home.

By Labor Day I was thinner—thin enough to face the lobby mirror without flinching—but the pounds I had starved off slowly reappeared in October. By November they were all back. I was ashamed of my non-existent will power, and when I spotted Marlene on a street corner one day, I turned and walked the other way.

I had been a member of the Madison Chorus for three years when I graduated in 1954. It was a school tradition to award medals to its most outstanding members. Marlene got one. So did a few other people whom I felt had average, even mediocre, voices. Yet Miss Stein, the greyish, spinsterish chorus teacher, saw fit to deny me the honour.

It was the day before graduation when I confronted her on the subject. 'I'm sorry, Al,' she said in a clipped voice. She had a thick Brooklyn accent and she affected a ludicrous, pseudo-British tone to disguise it. 'I didn't feel your work merited an award.'

'I sing better than anyone here.' Shock had stripped away my usual modesty.

'You have a better *voice*,' Miss Stein said. 'But you've been fooling around too much. You've disrupted the class on far too many occasions.'

'What does that have to do with my ability to sing?'

'Singing isn't everything.'

'It is in a chorus. It's not fair.'

I don't know why the medal meant so much. Maybe it was because my father had said, 'I'll eat my hat if you ever make it. You're no singer.'

'You have to learn to be part of an ensemble,' Miss Stein continued. 'And unfortunately, you're a show-off. You can't be better than a group if you're part of it. You have to blend in.'

'How will I ever be noticed if I blend in?'

She shrugged, as if talking to an idiot.

*Careful. Keep a lid on the anger.*

My hands were sweating. The palpitations I dreaded were already galloping in my chest.

*Be nice!*

'I deserve that medal. And you know something else? In five years I'm going to be famous, more famous than anybody in the rotten chorus.'

'Perhaps. If you learn discipline.'

'I deserve that medal,' I repeated.

In my frustration, I somehow hoped she would see the error of her ways and relent. She didn't. Shaken as she was, she stood her ground while I muttered, 'It's not fair,' over and over again.

# 4
# *Forced to Leave Home*

It was November 1958, and my bed was shaking. I felt fear even through the smothering curtain of sleep. Sounds tore at my ears: the clanging radiator, my father's roaring voice through the paper-thin walls, my mother's whining pleas, 'Irving, leave him alone.'

'Get up, damn it,' my father raged. 'Get out of bed, you bum!'

I couldn't seem to rouse myself. The alarm clock on the table said 6.30. 'You think you can stay out all night,' my father demanded, 'drinking and fooling about with your no-good friends?'

'I was working. Singing.'

'Singing? Is that what you call it? Singing?'

*Yes*, I thought. Singing for pennies at the Harbor Club in Staten Island, sailing back and forth on a ferry with Jack and our drummer and guitarist, pounding out standards for disinterested customers who had come to see Desiree, the club's featured stripper.

I had arrived home after four, desperate for sleep. Even the deafening sound of my father's snoring in the next room hadn't kept me up, as it usually did. 'You gonna wash the floors of the shop, big shot? Like you promised? *Big shot!*'

I buried my head in my pillow, unprepared for the bearded face, the bloodshot eyes, the sickening breath that smelled, more than ever, like sweet and sour vomit.

'I'll come downstairs when I'm ready,' I said. 'Please. . . .' always polite, even in jeopardy. . . . 'Please get out of my room for a minute.'

'Your room? Who the hell pays for this room—for the food you eat—so you can waste time messing around with your friends?'

I wanted to say: 'I pay for this room. I pay for my food. I've been working since I was seven years old; as a delivery boy, a busboy. At eight I had a paper round. At ten. . .'

*Be nice.*

'I said *get out of bed!*'

My vision was still foggy, but I looked up in time to see a mop handle bearing down on me. My father had torn the mop portion off.

I jumped out of the way and wood crashed into my yellow Emerson radio on the night table, cracking it in half.

It would have been my head.

He rushed towards the table that contained my records—a collection I treasured, with 78s by Perry Como, Frank Sinatra, Bing Crosby, Al Jolson and some of the new songs that were beginning to gain popularity—songs from the rock 'n' roll wave my parents and brother denounced as trash: 'Don't Be Cruel' by Elvis Presley, whom I had added to my list of imitations; 'Whole Lotta Shakin' Goin' On' by Jerry Lee Lewis. He was picking them up, bending them in half like a circus strong man, shattering the 78s to bits.

It was, finally, enough.

The rage I reserved for the football field exploded. I slammed my father against the wall. More surprise than pain showed on his face. 'Alfred,' my mother cried, 'don't hit your father.' Her voice was dim. My brain, in self-defence, had blotted out the incapacitating phrase, *Be nice.* I couldn't let him kill me.

But her cry had distracted me long enough to allow him to race to the kitchen and scoop a knife from the cutlery drawer. He came at me, grinning, chopping the air. The blade grazed my forehead.

I lunged, shoving him to the floor. The knife flew from his hand. We rolled around, pummelling each other. My youth, the years of suppressing hate for peace overwhelmed him. The wrestler from Poland was no match for twenty years of hate.

Blood squirted from his nose, and my fist kept hammering away. I felt something break. I wanted all his features to disintegrate into a sticky red pool. This time the police wouldn't have to come to protect me, to extricate me from an imprisoning wardrobe. I could take care of myself.

He was stretched out on the floor, moaning, semiconscious, when I fled. My mother called, 'Alfred, where are you going? Don't leave me with him,' but nothing could have stopped me. It was a bizarre scene; me racing down a Brooklyn street on a quiet Sunday morning, my mother running behind, sobbing, imploring. She must have known that unless she calmed me down, I would be gone for ever.

The distance between us grew wider. Her words were swallowed up in the sound of cabs and buses. Soon I was on a subway, shaking as violently as the train itself as it bounced along ageing tracks on the way to Manhattan.

I turned up at my brother's flat an hour later. I couldn't think of anywhere else to go.

Two years before, Larry had finally moved into a place of his own. In that time he had gained a good reputation as a stage manager, and was currently stage managing the hit Johnny Mercer musical L'il Abner. When Larry answered the door and saw his bloodied brother in the hall, he grew pale.

I had no suitcases, but he knew instantly that his privacy was about to be invaded. A part of the Brooklyn nightmare he had struggled to escape was crashing in on his hard-won turf.

Just then a tall, blond man in his early twenties emerged from Larry's room. All he had on was tight black briefs.

'Oh, Eric, this is my brother Al.'

'Hi.' Eric shook my hand heartily, trying to act as though the situation was completely natural. But he knew better. Larry had flashed him a look the minute he appeared; a look that said, 'Please get out!'

I was startled by Eric's arms, the thickest, most muscular arms I'd ever come across outside of a muscle magazine.

'Maybe I should come back tonight,' I suggested.

Although my brother was probably wishing I'd go away permanently, he disguised his feelings and tentatively hugged me. Eric vanished and returned a few minutes later, fully dressed. He said he looked forward to seeing me again and left, blowing Larry a kiss as he departed.

'Very theatrical, isn't he?' I said, to ease the tension.

'That's show biz. Now tell me everything.'

When I related the violent details, my brother waved them aside. 'It was probably just one of daddy's drunken fits. He's probably forgotten all about it by now.'

'Well I haven't,' I said. It struck me funny that Larry used the word 'daddy'.

'Where will you stay?'

'I thought . . .' OK, I'll ask. I'll swallow my pride. 'Here. . . till I find a place to live.'

I ached for a gesture from him. I wished he would welcome my presence.

'We'll see.'

Over the next few days, my mother called repeatedly. She begged me to come back. 'Your father is sorry,' she said. 'He loves you.'

'No, Mom.'

'L'Alfred, please!'

'*Alfred*, Mom.' I held my ground, despite the palpitations, rubbing my sweaty palms against the jeans I'd borrowed from my brother.

'You're making Mother miserable,' Larry said. 'I think you should go home and give it one more try.'

Gradually I got to meet Larry's friends, even though he did his best to keep them away from me—slim, brown-eyed Stan, a publicist at MGM; Mark, with his strange combination of closely-cropped blond hair and thick moustache, a costume designer making his way with low-budget off-Broadway shows; and Nathan, who wore a red bandanna and hat to cover his premature baldness.

They were all friendly and I talked freely to them, but it was uncomfortably evident that Larry wanted to discourage any contact. Without spelling it out, the message was: 'These are my friends. This is my world. You don't belong.'

Much as Larry tried to censor conversations, there was no way I could avoid piecing together random information. Eric was staying with another friend, but he had been Larry's secret flatmate before I arrived. Mark had been Larry's lover until Eric arrived on the scene, and he was for ever tossing poison verbal darts at Larry about it.

Stan, I slowly gathered, was juggling three lovers simultaneously and trying to figure out which one of the men he loved most.

Sleeping in Larry's bed, alone with my thoughts, I struggled to come to terms with my brother's homosexuality. I blamed my mother for her over-protectiveness; my father for his cruelty and violence.

I remembered my mother's constant refrain, 'Be like your brother,' and thought, 'No. . . I'm nothing like him.'

It was a relief when I moved to a friend's flat and escaped that environment. I knew it would take months, even years, to absorb the truth of my brother's life and place it all in perspective.

Free of my family and armed with the optimism and innocence of nineteen, I set out to conquer the world of music. Life on 49th and Broadway had to be easier than the tension and tyranny of Avenue M.

My first rude awakening took place in front of the Brill Building, 1619 Broadway. The Brill Building housed the majority of important New York publishers and song-writers. When I first approached the entrance, I was assaulted by hostile, repeated screaming. Startled, I turned to face an unshaved tramp who continued to shout, 'Drop dead. . . go to hell,' amid obscene noises. Trembling, I escaped into the building. I learned that the middle-aged tramp with the empty shopping bag was known as Broadway Larry, and everyone had to duck past his hostile ravings when-ever they entered the Brill.

I soon learned that Elvis Presley's music publishers, Hill and Range, were based in the Brill Building. Blues singers such as Chuck Berry and Muddy Waters were signed to a Brill Building publisher, Merrimac Music. Shortly afterwards I became familiar with the other half of the publishing/ song-writing world across the street at 1650 Broadway. This building was the home of Don Kirshner, a boy genius who had already signed several of my Brooklyn class-mates: Barry Mann, Neil Sedaka, Howie Greenfield and Carole King.

Unfortunately he didn't sign me. He did, however, ask me to sit down and write a song for Connie Francis, then at her hottest. I felt encouraged, till I realised that every one of his writers was competing for the same session. That was Kirshner's method: to give all his staff writers an assignment, stir up fierce competition. A smash hit inevitably emerged.

Everyone remembers those days through a rosy, romantic haze. It's true we were all young, feverishly committed and full of dreams; but the battles were emotionally wrenching. Jack Keller admitted, after the Brill Building days were over, that he suffered nightmares all the time, hearing the voice of Kirshner, the benevolent but driving father, pushing him to *produce*. And then the sense of loss when 'father' withdrew, and the singer-songwriter changed the course of the industry.

The demonstration record I made didn't help either. I had recorded a piano-voice rendition that sounded empty next to the fully produced and orchestrated demos my peers were making. My brother lent me some money, even though he despised rock 'n' roll and thought only theatre music had merit. Eric pushed him on my behalf, and even slipped me a few dollars of his own.

I guaranteed them that 'Blue Tears' was perfect for Connie Francis and would be a Number One. I guess my youthful fervour convinced them—or they were just being kind.

A year later, when I listened to 'Blue Tears' again, I knew just how kind they had been.

By then my naivete had faded, but not my optimism. I knew the joy of getting an 'A' side, only to be told by the producer that the record 'didn't turn out well; we're putting it in the can'. Which meant permanently shelved.

I knew that forcing my way through a few doors and getting songs published was simply the first step in a long road towards making the charts.

Worst of all, I knew the feeling of going on Billboard's Hot 100 (at 99), staying there a second week, and falling off.

The publishers were a varied bunch. Some were heavy, with dark, intimidating cigars. Others wore custom-made suits and slicked their hair straight back. Some, or so went the whispers, were 'mafioso'; others were gay. But all of them, in the 1960s, had one thing in common: a sharp, nearly infallible song sense. They went out there and courted artists, wined and dined producers, did *anything* to get the record.

They also gave advances—usually $50.00—to freelance writers when they liked a song. The advances were never enough to cover expenses, but they kept me going.

I continued to move from one friend's place to another, intermittently returning to Larry. The money struggles were frustrating, but not as frustrating as the awareness of my contemporaries securing a firm hold on the charts. Barry Mann (who became my flatmate for six months before marrying Cynthia Weil) already had 'Who Put the Bomp', and Neil Sedaka was a success with 'My Diary'. Carole King and Gerry Goffin had electrified the industry with 'Will You Love Me Tomorrow?'.

The other side of the coin was equally disconcerting: observing those who tried and failed, who became waiters, clerks, anything to stay in, to realise their dreams. Some were just a few years older than I, others were middle-aged, discouraged but persistent. They were the group who had had some success, but had been cheated of royalties. Or they were the 'one-hit wonders', who never followed up after a chart bull's-eye. The ones who had had that taste, that isolated charge, had been sentenced to a lifetime of effort and false hope.

As I ploughed along, I was also unjustly deprived of royal-ties. On one occasion, I learned this through a secretary; but when I pressed a day later for more information, she turned white and said it was a 'mistake'. Her boss had obviously spoken to her.

I was too poor to involve a lawyer and incur legal fees—fees that would sap the royalties in question if I ever collected them.

In my lowest moments, I had nightmares that I would move back to Brooklyn or turn to my parents for money. I heard my father's voice, 'You'll never make it,' and wondered if he was right. Songs poured out; songs I rewrote endlessly and put on demos. With each one I thought, 'This is it,' until it was rejected a few weeks later.

'Not right for Connie.'

'Dion's going in a different direction.'

'The Shirelles don't want ballads, they want up-tempo songs.' I wrote with a dozen collaborators during this period, searching for that strange, indefinable chemistry that Goffin and King had, or Sedaka and Greenfield. It never seemed to happen.

Still, the occasional record was exciting, and the heated competition stirred up my creative juices. I learned to make polished demos, the kind Kirshner demanded from Barry, Neil and the rest of his staff. I would often sing lead and all the harmony parts; anything to save money, yet make a demo sound full on a minuscule budget. My skills as an impressionist helped too. I imitated artists such as Bobby Darin and Jackie Wilson, and they did the songs because they were so flattered by my imitations. Jackie Wilson's publisher, Arc-Merrimac, kept me busy writing for Jackie's dates.

Good fortune smiled when Roulette Records volunteered to produce four sides with me. The 'A' side was a deathless item entitled '49 Jukeboxes', co-authored by Lee Morris of 'Velvet' fame.

'49 Jukeboxes' failed to enhance Morris' career or mine, though it was picked by *Cashbox* and *Billboard*. Discriminating disc jockeys and record buyers were less impressed, and my name, Alfy Weatherbee, didn't help. It was the era of Buddys, Bobbys and Frankies. Alfy had seemed appropriate.

Personal appearances included Dick Clark's *American Bandstand*, and Roulette sent me on a tour with Jimmy Bowen (who had the hit 'I'm Stickin' With You'), Buddy Knox ('Party Doll'), and other lesser-known names like myself. The performing was fun, the interludes between shows boring. Some performers plugged up the gaps with gambling, drinking and drugs. Even then hotel rooms were wrecked. Vicious arguments would erupt among group members due to tension and lack of sleep.

I never drank; I think I feared the loss of control. I did, however, fall into the familiar role of listening to the problems of other singers and musicians. Listening to others' problems eased the isolation, made me feel useful and made me more comfortable about refusing the sensual temptations constantly being tossed my way.

I tried to help junkies and alcoholics, sometimes holding their hands for hours. Often I dried their tears. I had no formal speeches or advice to give them, but I instinctively knew what to say to bring temporary comfort. Occasionally their anger would spill out, even at me; and I would do what I could to give them a sense of worth, a sense that life still held good things if they kept trying.

Extending to people what I had always yearned for—a loving and supportive parent—is what bolstered my own sense of self-worth. By becoming a parent to those in need I became, in a sense, my own parent—what the organisation for recovered alcoholics and their families, Al-Anon, refers to as 'parenting yourself'.

Dealing with alcoholics presented a challenge. I thought of my father, especially when a twenty-year-old bass player admitted that he often got drunk and beat his wife. My first impulse was to lash out, to scream: 'Do you know what you're doing? Do you know the pain you're inflicting on your family?' I sat rigid, bit my tongue, and held my temper in. It was important to understand the bass player's suffering; important to project into his troubled soul and glimpse the self-hatred and guilt.

A drummer with a group called 'The Hollywood Flames' dubbed me Preacher. A black backing singer tagged me Father Al and the name stuck. Father Al, and only twenty-one years old!

Somehow I earned enough money to keep going. I worked at weekends as an impressionist when the '49 Jukeboxes' tour ended. Jack Keller and I continued to entertain at Jewish community affairs, and I was paid minimal wages to cut demos of songs Barton Music published, written by other people. A follow-up record was released, 'String Along with Pearl'. No one strung along with Alfy on that one either.

When I met Jean O'Hara she was thirty-two, ten years older than I was. She worked as a secretary at Warner Brothers and was sympathetic to my struggles. Her eyes were pale blue with premature lines underneath them— the result of too many late nights. Jean lived on Central Park West with her sister Harriett.

This was during a period when I had run out of couches and was back with Larry. I confided my frustration that I had nowhere to live. 'Why not move in with me for a while?' Jean offered. She said it casually, making it simple for me to accept or reject the invitation. I didn't know what I felt about Jean, beyond a strong physical attraction, but I said 'yes'.

The situation made me feel daring and excitingly grown-up. I was sleeping with a much older woman. Not only that, but her sister had a fondness for black musicians, and she lived, on and off, with two—Joe Jones, a drummer with Count Basie's band, and Howard McGee, a jazz trumpet player. (I never met their other sister, a nun.)

Howard quickly became my friend. He had faced a lifetime of hard knocks, including an addiction to heroin, and had evolved a philosophy that helped him to cope.

'You know, Al,' he once said, as we stood in front of our fifth-floor window overlooking the park. 'I'm a black man. I've been on heroin. I've been higher than a bird, lower than any gutter. But see these buildings?' His long, dark finger indicated a high-rise in the distance. 'A lot of buildings are being torn down, but remember, a lot of new ones keep going up.'

The optimistic truth of that statement, its positiveness in the face of Howard's misspent life, gave me a fresh charge of hope. So what if I'd had a couple of duff records? I was only twenty-one; I had no right to feel discouraged.

I also identified with Howard's other statement: 'You know why black people sing so loud in church? 'Cause they're afraid the Lord ain't hearin' them.'

Except that Howard believed the Lord *was* hearing him. 'Jesus is always there,' he said, and when he spoke a light seemed to erase the lines of pain and hard living that creased his face.

Howard's belief in Jesus, in view of his troubles, amazed me. He made God sound like his best friend, someone loving and ever-present. I had always thought of God as caring, but far out of reach—not someone I could touch. My friendship with Howard reinforced a feeling I'd always had, of being completely at ease with black people. I had none of my father's bigotry. Black people possessed a marvellous freedom, an unself-conscious, pulsating energy and passion that was appealing to a Jewish boy whose stomach had been tied up in knots all his life. They laughed easily; expressed emotions with spontaneity. They appeared to be more comfortable with sex than any of my Jewish friends.

Including me. I felt guilty everytime Jean and I made love. I knew I didn't really want to. A stubborn romantic streak in me rebelled at the looseness, the lack of commitment. The lack, fundamentally, of real caring.

But I thought: 'I should find this exciting. I want to be "in", "cool", "with it".' My friends would have laughed at me for the old-fashioned thoughts I was having. They already laughed at me when I didn't get drunk or try the numerous drugs that were always being passed around.

Jean laughed too at the discomfort I occasionally showed about our living arrangements. 'Forget what you see in Disney films,' she said. 'This is real life.'

I went along with it, uneasily. The best part of the whole set-up continued to be my talks with Howard. He opened

my eyes to great black entertainers: the silky magic of Sam
Cooke, the wit of Chuck Berry, the pounding piano of Fats
Domino. I still played soundtracks of *My Fair Lady* and
*West Side Story*; still worshipped Rodgers and Hammerstein (quietly). Jean hated their squeaky-clean 'shmaltz',
but I was learning that an affection for one kind of music
doesn't preclude appreciating another.

I was embarking, at last, on the one consistent, never-
ending love affair of my life: writing. I still clung to dreams
of singing stardom, but they were beginning to recede. I
was overcome with a need to convey everything I felt and
saw—the beauty and ugliness, the loneliness and hope, all
shades of human feeling. My own emotions followed a
roller-coaster course, up and down, unable to settle on
anything; but the ride was exhilarating and I yearned to
give it creative shape. Howard introduced me to a highly
respected black writer, Luther Dixon. Luther had written
'Sixteen Candles' and 'Why Baby Why' and had a golden
commercial touch. A few of our songs were recorded
immediately. None was a hit, but I felt sure I was on the
verge of a breakthrough.

Luther took me to Adam Clayton Powell's Abyssinian
Church in Harlem. It was my first exposure to a church
that seemed to rock with a passion for God; a passion that
rose from stamping feet, clapping hands and voices raised
straight to heaven. The pianist wasn't reproducing hymns.
He was making an urgent personal statement, a statement
taken up by the men, women and children who sang their
souls out. 'Thank you, Jesus, thank you, Father, thank
you,' the voices cried in frenzied unison. I felt, for that
moment, part of something much bigger than I had ever
known. They sang a hymn 'Standing in the Need of a
Prayer'. I was so mesmerised by the melody that I put my
own lyrics to it, 'Sing and Tell the Blues So Long'. When
Jackie Wilson later recorded it, I felt no guilt about the secular rewrite. It was a joyous tune that could move people,

make them feel good, and give them a sense of belief in the future.

Luther and the promise of songwriting success carried me through my next personal crisis. Jean and I met, at her insistence, in front of Jack Dempsey's Restaurant on 49th Street, and she told me I would have to move out. 'I'm older than you,' she said, her lined, blue-grey eyes apologetic. But I knew better. Howard had tipped me off that Jean was now involved with a black bass player.

I didn't see Howard for a year. When I ran into him, he admitted that he had gone back on heroin, then kicked it again. 'Remember the new buildings,' he reminded me, hugging me with gruff, reassuring warmth.

I worked feverishly. Luther was hard to pin down; he was an undisciplined genius and only wrote when he was in the mood, usually at two or three in the morning. I kept after him, more aware than ever that my Brooklyn friends had the charts almost sewn up. Neil and Barry were now taking turns at Number One. Even my old Catskills buddy, Jack Keller, had a hit, 'Just Between You and Me', by the Chordettes. I couldn't fall behind.

# 5
# Negative Voices

Happiness is a mystery, a kind of optimistic, untroubled state that springs from a healthy self-image. If you feel you *deserve* happiness, you'll stand a much better chance of being happy. Otherwise you'll twist even good things into negatives so you can suffer.

If someone had said to me in 1960 that I wanted to suffer, I'd have stared at them uncomprehendingly. Hadn't I suffered enough? I'd paid my dues with an unstable childhood. I'd grown up in poverty. From now on, all I wanted was harmony and peace.

For all my self-analysing, it didn't occur to me that I felt unworthy; that I deliberately set out to wreck any harmony and peace that came my way. In work I suffered because I never felt I was doing enough, even when I hit a lucky streak. In relationships I zeroed in on the most unsuitable, unavailable women—women who could be relied upon to disrupt my life.

My tendency in that direction reached its height when I met my first wife, Felicia.

Felicia was eighteen at the time; I was twenty-two. Attractive, blonde and a cross between actress Nina Foch and Susan Oliver, she was bright and opinionated. She was also going out with my friend Noel Goldstein.

Noel was like Barry: slim and handsome, another Boy-Most-Likely-to-Succeed. I was flattered that Felicia seemed to prefer me. Unlike Marlene, she was choosing the underdog. I was still chubby, still alternating between crash diets (accompanied by excessive pill taking) and middle-of-the-night ice cream snacks.

On our second date, we went to the Avalon Theatre in Brooklyn to see Rita Hayworth's *The Story on Page One*. A song of Luther's and mine, 'Irresistible You', was climbing the charts with Bobby Darin, and we talked a great deal about my musical ambitions. A top publisher, Merrimac Music (managers of Jackie Wilson), wanted to sign me to a writer's contract. I was gratified that Felicia seemed to take joy in my success.

We became lovers that night.

Maybe the relationship could have developed into something meaningful and lasting. As it turned out, her mother called only weeks later. When I said 'hello', there was a silence, followed by three angry words: 'Felicia is pregnant.'

It's strange; I didn't lash out, didn't fight back. I accepted the situation as my due. It didn't matter that the freedom I had finally tasted, away from the constricting controls of my parents, was about to be stolen. I experienced the calmness of a man on his way to the electric chair.

The only person I confided in was my brother, and he begged me to reconsider. For once I felt warmth and concern from him.

'You don't love this girl. . . you don't even know her,' he said. 'And what about your career? You're just getting started.'

'I have no choice.'

'There's always a choice,' Larry said. 'Have you thought about abortion?'

'I can't.'

Larry's face changed. It tightened, closed up, shutting me out. That rare glimpse of warmth was gone. 'Then why ask for my advice when you've already made up your mind?'

Before we could talk any more, my parents arrived. It was Father's Day, and we were following our annual ritual of taking my father out to lunch at the Plaza. Larry dreaded this; appearances mattered desperately to him, and he was always afraid of running into theatre people he knew. My father, on his best days, spoke too loudly and for too long, calling attention to himself, making fun of the waiters or complaining about the service.

I sensed disaster the minute I noticed my father's face. His eyes were red; he looked unshaven. His walk was unsteady.

'My two sons,' he boomed, causing nearby heads to turn. 'Father's Day with my two sons.'

'I can't take this,' Larry whispered to me. 'I really can't.'

'Now, Irving, just sit down,' said my mother, ever the peacemaker.

'Don't tell me what to do,' my father said harshly.

Like an unruly, rebellious child, my father took gleeful pleasure in tormenting all of us, particularly Larry. He ordered one drink, then another. And he sent back the first thing he ordered, a salad, complaining that the lettuce was old and wilted.

'They don't serve bad lettuce at the Oak Room,' I said.

'It stinks,' my father said. 'It's stale. Look at it!'

Larry stood up. 'I think we'd better go.'

'Sit down,' said my father. 'Sit down and show some respect. It's Father's Day.'

By now the entire restaurant was watching. Another salad was brought and my father took a few bites. But the main course—roast beef—was too rare. In a drunken rage, he threw it on the floor, smashing the plate to bits.

A gasp filled the Oak Room.

'Irving, please, stop it,' cried my mother, sounding pathetic and ineffectual. 'Larry... Alfred... he doesn't mean it. He's just not himself today.'

'He's like this every day!' Larry said, gnashing his teeth.

By now the disturbance was too great to be ignored, and the maître d' came over to our table. He was sorry, he hated to do this, but he had to ask us to leave. Yes, he knew that Larry was a good customer, and it was nothing personal, but his other customers were becoming upset. . .

Minutes later we were in the lobby. My brother's face was flushed. I couldn't tell whether he wanted to cry or scream with rage—probably both.

'I have rotten sons,' my father said. 'Two rotten sons. You let them throw me out. Maybe I'm not good enough for your fancy restaurants, huh? Maybe I'm not good enough for the great Larry Kasha. . . my great fairy of a son, Larry Kasha! Fairy boy, fairy boy. . . .'

Larry flung my father against a wall, and the two of them pounded away at each other while my mother sobbed. I did my best to pull them apart. It wasn't easy. My brother's exercising and weight-lifting had made him powerful—just as powerful as my father.

All my strength was required, in addition to the efforts of a doorman and a passerby, to yank the two apart. It was clear that this was a fight to the death—that they wanted to kill each other, nothing less.

Larry backed away and left the scene. My father kept calling after him, 'Rotten son. . . rotten no good fairy.'

Then, mercifully, he passed out.

I barely had time to recover from the trauma of that day when I was hurled back into the reality of my situation with Felicia. Despite Larry's advice, I saw no exit, no escape hatch. It didn't matter that Felicia was little more than a stranger. I was saddling myself with a wife—a woman I barely knew—and a child. I was almost broke; record royalties for 'Irresistible You' wouldn't be coming in for another nine months to a year. The Merrimac contract might mean future security, but I had no guarantee that my contract would be extended after the first year. I was twenty-two years old, in a notoriously insecure business.

But there it was. I wanted to do the right thing.

We decided to be married secretly so that my parents would have adequate time to accept the decision. In February we would dance through the ritual of a large wedding at the New York Hotel on 34th Street. Despite everything they had done, I was afraid of displeasing them. Getting married young was bad enough from my mother's point of view. Doing it without any interval of preparation would have been a heinous crime. Ironically, a month after our secret wedding, Felicia suffered a miscarriage. Plans moved ahead for our second ceremony, even though my mother received an anonymous note, informing her that Felicia and I were already married. She was enraged and hurt. And for once my parents were united in something: their anger towards me.

I never found out who sent the note. It was pieced together with letters from a newspaper. When bitterness began to overwhelm our marriage, I speculated that Felicia might have done it.

In any case, it was a bad start. The wedding was a disaster. My mother wore a heartbroken expression throughout (clearly shown in the family snapshots). She later admitted that the marriage 'nearly killed her'. Felicia's parents regarded me as a villain for what I had done to their daughter. Pictures of me reveal an unsmiling, heavy-set groom. They don't reveal the panic symptoms that were now becoming familiar: shortness of breath, drenched palms and an overwhelming urge to hide. The previous night, after lying dormant for years, my wardrobe nightmare had returned. But this time I was bigger, and my body had become wedged between the walls of the wardrobe. Movement became impossible, until the only recourse was to beat my head against the door, smashing my skull.

My father's insistence on cutting my hair for the wedding was another bad omen; it brought back the bar mitzvah. 'Promise you won't make it too short,' I had said, but he scalped me, probably in revenge for growing long hair as soon as I was free of him. 'See, Rose?' he said, pointing with pride to my shorn skull, as if to announce, 'They're *my* sons too!'

The only saving grace was Jackie Wilson, whom I had come to know as a friend. Jackie volunteered to sing, and his touching rendition of 'Danny Boy' moved nearly everyone to tears. Everyone, of course, except my father, who wondered loudly, 'What's that *schvartze* doing here?'

'Daddy, that's a famous star. That's Jackie Wilson,' I said, trying desperately to shut him up.

'He's still a black man.'

'Daddy!'

'He's a *schvartze*.'

When they were introduced, he crushed Jackie's knuckles. Jackie didn't flinch; his expression remained polite, but he squeezed my father's fingers with answering tightness. I saw those drink-reddened eyes widen with shock. I held my breath. My father was competing, applying more pressure. Jackie grinned. What my father didn't know was that Jackie had once been a Golden Gloves champ and his grip was still powerful.

'You're wearing a Jewish star. Why?'

'Because I'm Jewish,' said Jackie.

'You're Jewish? A *schvartze*? Jewish?'

'My dad's a rabbi.'

'*Ha!*'

'Irving,' my mother said, pulling him away. I noticed him moving his fingers and wincing; Jackie had hurt him.

'I'm sorry,' I said to Jackie. 'When he gets drunk. . .'

'It's OK, man. I understand.'

I wished *I* did.

The pattern of my married life can best be expressed by mentioning the film Felicia and I went to see on our wedding night: *Psycho*.

Felicia and I tried to make a go of a difficult situation. We found a flat on Central Park West and her parents, reconciled now to our marriage, helped with the down payment. I had a record in the Top 10 with Jackie, 'My Empty Arms', co-written with Hank Hunter.

I was still trying to be a singer, so when Jackie went on tour and asked me to be part of the performing package, I jumped at the chance. I hadn't forgotten my distaste for the road, but it meant freedom, a chance to think about my marriage, to sort it out.

I enjoyed touring more this time, principally because Jackie was the headliner. I was his greatest fan; I worshipped his talent. In my opinion, no one has ever had the charisma, the energy, the sheer unrestrained magnetism that Jackie had on stage. (Michael Jackson today credits Wilson as his greatest influence.) Women went into hysterics. His teenage experience as a boxer accounted for his aggressive grace and body language and breathtaking agility while dancing. He projected raw sex and high spirits.

Most of all, though, he had a fantastic vocal instrument; a voice that encompassed operatic notes and rhythmic curls with equal ease. I felt an incredible pride that this rock 'n' roll great was doing *my* songs. Until then his hits had been penned by Berry Gordy ('Lonely Teardrops' and 'That's Why'), but Gordy, following a run-in with Jackie's manager, had left the office. Shortly after, Gordy established Motown Records. Jackie always spoke of Gordy's songwriting talent with awe, and I felt privileged to follow in his footsteps.

Jackie's Judaism gave us a basic bond. We spent endless hours talking about faith, about the need for a spiritual anchor. We agreed that God provided a balance against the shabby underside of show business: disloyal co-workers, thieving managers and publishers, hangers-on, record company prejudice.

And the prejudice wasn't just confined to record companies. In Alabama, white kids started throwing things at Jackie on stage. Mississippi was worse, when a group of trouble-makers screamed out, 'Stop the nigger music!'

I was put up at fine hotels; Jackie and the other black members of the tour were forced to stay in run-down, second-rate hovels.

Prayer was a vital protection, and whenever we could, we'd pray or go to a synagogue. We also went to the cinema and concerts. We met after shows and took walks to unwind. Jackie was warm, considerate and loving, but his personal excesses warred with the spiritual side of his nature.

In February, his womanising backfired when a twenty-eight-year-old woman turned up at his flat and tried to persuade him to make love to her. He refused, and she pulled out a gun. In the ensuing struggle, Jackie was shot and seriously wounded. He was bleeding profusely, but luckily his flat was only a block from Roosevelt Hospital. The quick availability of medical help saved his life.

I went to the hospital and tried to offer words of encouragement. I even prayed for him, though I was still self-conscious about it; still searching for the proper 'exact' mode of expression. I didn't know yet that prayer has no rules—except that you say what you truly feel; what is in your heart. But Jackie thanked me and said it helped.

Gene Goodman was also at his bedside, and in typical publisher fashion, he said, 'OK, we need a song to bring Jackie back. Got any ideas?' I went home and wrote 'I'm Comin' on Back to You', which Jackie cut as soon as he was out of hospital. It became a Top 10 record, and he was bigger than ever.

I doubt if Jackie ever found personal peace. At that time, the early 1960s, I didn't think I ever would either. I worried incessantly: Would the hit records stop? Would I ever have a hit as a singer? Would my parents and brother approve? Would I ever make a success of my marriage? *Keep trying.*

*Run faster. Out-race the negative voices.*

In early 1962, I became friendly with a gregarious, out-going music publisher I'll call Carl. I knew Carl was married, but few people had ever met his wife and no one mentioned her. There seemed to be an unspoken agreement to omit her name from any conversation.

My curiosity prompted me to ask around. I learned that the missing wife never left her home. She had, in fact, existed in self-imposed isolation for twelve years. Nothing could wrench her from the safety of her three-room harbour. 'I've heard of *housewives*,' one friend of mine joked, 'but this is carrying it too far.' The attitudes varied from 'she must be crazy' and 'maybe she's a phantom' to 'I bet old Carl keeps her tied up'. Nobody demonstrated any compassion for a human being so troubled that she lacked the courage to walk down the street.

I remember feeling a shiver of empathy. I had no idea why at the time. It was my first brush with agoraphobia, and I experienced a wave of fear and a desire to shut the situa-tion out of my mind. To combat my mysterious, unaccountable reaction, I decided to drop in on Carl one Saturday. I located his flat on West End Avenue and rang the doorbell.

'Hello?' A high-pitched, tremulous voice fluttered through the intercom. 'Who is it?'

'Al Kasha. Is Carl there?'

'No.' She sounded frightened.

'Could I. . .' But before I finished, she cut me off. I was reluctant to leave. Just then, a tenant came down and the door to the main entrance swung open. I hurried inside and climbed three flights of stairs to Carl's flat. I rang the bell. The same muffled bird-like voice greeted me from behind a thick, discoloured door.

'This is Al Kasha,' I said. 'I'm a friend of Carl's.'

'Please go away,' the woman begged. 'Carl will be home later. *Please.*'

'I'd like to talk to you.' The compulsion to help pushed

me on, even though I felt guilty about alarming her and invading her territory. 'I'll call the police.' Her words were bold, but the pitiful tone stayed the same. 'I'll call the police right now.' She began to dial.

I had no choice but to leave.

Instinctively I understood her dread of leaving the flat. I was already beginning to suffer similar feelings. Even then, I picked places where I could be comfortable, and nothing could prise me from them. When I met with writing collaborators, I fought to arrange the sessions on my turf. Once I'd chosen a relaxed place, I conducted business there, ate there, stayed there until late at night. The New York streets were suddenly threatening, and sometimes I took cabs to avoid walking a few blocks to my house. Impatience—anxiety—in restaurants began to surface and I hurried through meals, or asked for the bill before my main course was half finished. I claimed to hate dessert (although I ate compulsively at home) so I could leave quickly.

These phobic feelings were inconsistent in my twenties. Sometimes they would loom up with terrifying power; other times they diminished and disappeared. The same syndrome that made it impossible for me to sleep (anticipatory anxiety) now ruled my waking life. I avoided situations that *might* prove threatening: lifts, crowded supermarkets. I could control what happened to me on my own ground, nowhere else.

Felicia's possessiveness aggravated the tension. The more I clung to the liferaft of workaholism, the harder she held on. Looking back, I can't blame her. I was an inattentive husband, verbally and physically. We never touched. I retreated into my private thoughts, and she criticised and needled me to make contact.

Under happier circumstances, she might have been an invaluable help in my struggle, if I had only let her in. But I couldn't.

I followed trends, seeking to learn, to find a 'handle', a permanent answer that would guarantee continued success. I saw Bob Dylan in his early days at Gerde's Folk City in Greenwich Village. His voice and appearance were odd, but I recognised something brilliant and innovative in his music. I had an open mind to folk (as symbolised by the Kingston Trio), tearful Connie Francis rock ('My Heart Has a Mind of Its Own', written by Jack Keller and Howie Greenfield), and of course, the R & B represented by Jackie, Brook Benton, Hank Ballard and Jerry Butler.

Records were also an effective way of maintaining marital peace. The constant blast of music in our flat prevented hostile confrontations. In its absence, TV took over.

# 6

## Up the CBS Ladder

My career continued on an upward curve. Columbia Records (influenced by a recommendation from my friend George Alpert, owner of *Cashbox* magazine) asked me to sign as a staff producer. They had heard, and been impressed by, demos I'd produced for Merrimac, as well as my hit recordings. It was an incredible plum for an inexperienced twenty-three-year-old.

*'Don't do it!'*

The lone, dissenting voice came from Phil Spector, a musical legend as writer and producer, later to be dubbed by Thomas Wolfe as 'the tycoon of teen'.

'It'll ruin you. Rock 'n' roll is rhythm and blues. It's what you've been doing with Jackie Wilson. Not "Sing Along with Mitch" and all that junk. CBS is white man's land. That's not rock music.'

I didn't take him seriously for a minute—not even when Mitch Miller himself said, 'These rock 'n' roll kids are the worst. If I have to record people who sing no better than the kid next door, I don't want to record anybody. Vic Damone and Tony Bennett—now *they* can sing.'

CBS, whatever the drawbacks, was power, prestige and a lucrative salary. And I couldn't help thinking: 'Larry would approve of this. He would be proud of me.'

My father said, 'Are you sure they mean it?' and my mother cautioned me: 'Don't upset anybody. Just be nice, do your work and stay out of people's way.'

I was given Steve Lawrence and Eydie Gorme to produce. Both were initially reluctant to work with 'that kid',
but they finally consented. I turned to old friends Carole
King and Gerry Goffin, and they came through with 'Go
Away, Little Girl' for Steve. Barry Mann and Cynthia Weil
submitted another smash, 'Blame It on the Bossa Nova',
for Eydie. During this period I socialised constantly with
both couples. We all had an overriding drive in common. I
filled them in on my daily activities, letting them know
which artists were available.

Sometimes, though not often in those pre-singer/
songwriter days, an artist wrote for himself. Neil Diamond
was an example. I produced Neil's first record, 'Clown
Town'. His voice was a strikingly individual instrument; it
had a highly charged, compelling timbre that conveyed
both sexuality and emotion.

Neil and Columbia parted shortly afterwards, but years
later, in one of the typical ironies of show business, they re-
signed him for $6 million. I also became a big fan of
another Columbia artist, Bob Dylan. The company wanted
to drop Dylan. His first album had sold a paltry 4,000
copies. 'He doesn't have a great voice,' said one executive.

'Forget his voice,' I said. 'Listen to those *songs*. He's
going to be the biggest writer in the country one day.' I
later learned my intervention was a factor in their decision
to keep Dylan on the Columbia list.

The label *did* believe in Aretha Franklin, but they saw
her as an elegant, sophisticated Nancy Wilson type. When
Aretha's producer and discoverer, John Hammond, fell ill,
she was placed in my hands.

I thought of Phil Spector's warning: 'It's white man's
land.' Funky rhythm and blues material was out of the
question. Yet the songs had to be exciting. They had to
showcase her animal energy and strength.

The answer presented itself when I saw her perform
'Rock a Bye Your Baby' at the Village Vanguard in Green-

wich Village. Her father, Reverend C.L. Franklin, a giant on the gospel circuit and later a Chess recording star, had always encouraged Aretha's ambitions; and he involved himself strongly in the selection of her material. I found myself sweating when he stared piercingly in my direction and asked, 'What do you think of that?' The song was an oddball by commercial standards. I felt the Reverend's eyes measuring me, but I said, 'I think it ought to be her next record.' The man whose powerful voice could explode a church shook my hand heartily and said, 'Good for you.'

My boss, Dave Kapralik, didn't see it the Reverend's way. He was apoplectic. 'A *black* singer, and you cut her on an Al Jolson song!' Trembling inside, I stuck to my guns. 'I think it's a hit.'

'It had better be—or you're out of a job.'

'Rock a Bye Your Baby' was the first major success of Aretha Franklin's recording career, and the only Top 40 single she had with Columbia before her string of successes on Atlantic. The song had a basic power, enabling her to release the drive that had been hidden under ornate arrangements and timid, bland melodies.

Aretha also cut a song of mine that became a Number One R & B hit, 'Operation Heartbreak'. The song reflected my personal tensions at the time, and Aretha captured all the pain I had felt while writing it. What I observed in Aretha was the split that can exist in a performer's personality. Off-stage she was, by her own admission, 'shy'; but a wild, unrestrained quality surfaced in front of audiences. Any fears she had melted away.

Watching Aretha made me long for the release I had experienced while touring with Jackie. Without the outlet of performing, all my tensions went unreleased, turning back inside myself.

I tried to learn from everyone. The journey took me from the hard-hitting world of Aretha and Reverend Franklin to the studied elegance of CBS Records' president Goddard Lieberson. I took note of his polished, sophisticated style, his custom-made suits, the fine wines he drank.

I never found him alone in his office; a tailor would be constantly in attendance, altering a jacket or a pair of trousers. Lieberson had a satiric way of making his importance known: 'All great men are dead, and I'm feeling a little sickly myself' was a typical remark.

Lieberson defined rock as 'pre-puberty singers singing about post-puberty problems'. But he was a man of artistic taste and vision. He signed Barbra Streisand against the advice of those who thought her uncommercial. I knew Barbra slightly because my brother was the associate director of *Funny Girl*, and I knew her relentless quest for perfection. I dropped in on one of her recording sessions and saw the same quality emerge. 'It's not *there*,' she repeated. The arranger kept changing notes, switching unisons to harmonies and back again.

'What do you think, Al?' she asked suddenly. 'Which take was better: the last one or the one before?'

I volunteered an opinion. 'Maybe,' was her reply. 'But I want to play them back one more time.'

Some of the musicians were intimidated, obviously impatient. I knew how gruelling her perfectionist tendencies were, but I couldn't fault her. In the end the albums she did were brilliant, and that was all that counted.

I cut a Number One album, 'Winners', with Steve. Driven on by my own standards, and further influenced by Barbra's unwavering intensity, I worked all night and returned to the studio at eight in the morning. Felicia complained bitterly that she never saw me.

Overdubbing, mixing, listening again and again—I don't know how I found the energy. I heard my mother's voice, 'Remember, Alfred, a man is nothing if he's not a success.' The phrase *'You're nothing. You're nothing'* beat like a drum in my head.

It wasn't enough to have a hit. As Lionel Richie put it years later: 'Say I've come off a big album; the new one I'm cutting now has to be just as good. And I have to write the next one making sure that's as strong as the first two.'

Engineer Roy Hallee (later producer of Simon and Garfunkel) would listen as I muttered: 'Not enough bass, not enough drum, too much piano.' Finally, at five in the morning, he would comment, 'I thought I was bad, but you're insane.'

Gratification came when 'Go Away, Little Girl' hit Number One and 'Blame It on the Bossa Nova' was Number Five in the same week. A call from Quincy Jones also buoyed my spirits. Quincy, a superb arranger and producer, had a fantastic ear; and when he had difficulty identifying the instrumental sound used on 'Go Away, Little Girl', I felt I had accomplished something innovative and unusual. The instrument was actually Steve's whistle, speeded up.

My brother took my parents and me to Sardi's for a celebration. I was rattling on, permitting my elation to pour over. For once my psychological boxing gloves weren't on, so I was unprotected when my mother asked, 'I know you have all these hits, but do they like you? Do they really like you, L'Alfred?'

'*Alfred*, Mum.'

In retrospect the question seems silly, too silly to dwell upon, but it filled me with fear.

*Be nice.*

'Of course they like me,' I said. But I wasn't sure they really did—as if it mattered anyway. The chain reaction of doubts began: Do they respect me? Do they know how much I contributed? Would they want to work with me again?

I coped with the dinner by having four portions of ice cream. When I got home, I spent the whole night being sick.

In late 1962, I spent an evening with a woman who was to alter the course of my life. The evening was a brief, memorable ray of sunshine in the growing darkness of those anxious days.

Her name was Ceil, and she worked for a publishing firm called Shapiro Bernstein. Ceil was officially a secretary, but her boss (Leon Brettler, who ran the company) relied on her opinions about music and people. She possessed a rare, instinctive understanding of both. Her musical taste ran towards exciting, dance-oriented tunes, especially with a Latin flavour; she was a regular at the Palladium during the Tito Puente era. But she knew what was commercially strong, whether it came in the shape of 'Twist and Shout' by the Isley Brothers, or 'Roses Are Red' by Bobby Vinton.

Ceil always made me think of Gittel in *Two for the Seesaw*. She was small, with dark, beautiful eyes and a sparkling smile. Her slender, dancer-type body was always in motion, and even though she parted her dark hair conservatively in the middle, her fiery, expansive gestures and vigorous laughter suggested a free spirit.

I had talked to her on the phone many times, asking her to send Shapiro Bernstein material over to CBS for Steve and Eydie. I found myself calling more often than professionally necessary, and somehow I managed to invite her out to dinner.

We talked and talked, our conversation broken only once when Ceil stared in horror as I poured ketchup on my steak. In those years I poured ketchup on everything but ice cream.

Manhattan seemed intensely alive that night. The crowds, the lights, the towering buildings briefly became visions of promise, beautiful and beckoning and safe. I didn't think about running home, hiding, sneaking back into the cocoon of my office at CBS. I remember noticing a cinema where *The Days of Wine and Roses* was playing. I had suggested a film earlier, and that was one I wanted to see (I was drawn to all films about alcoholics), but I steered us past it. Our togetherness was too precious to be interrupted. And I talked about myself, my home life, my marriage, my frustration. I didn't feel the need, for once, to appear the confident, all-knowing parental figure. I opened up, fearlessly, astonished that I was doing it. We were walking by the East River when I said suddenly, 'I wonder how God makes sense of it all.'

'But he does,' Ceil responded with conviction. She took my hand. It was a gesture of warm, basic connection; the touch of a friend. But it was more. Her firm, spontaneous touch triggered off a hope I had hidden under my fanatic work drive. Her gesture suggested what was possible—the kind of love between a man and a woman I had yet to experience.

The water looked cold and black in the November night.

'I pray and he always hears me,' Ceil said simply.

Did he, I wondered? Ceil had suffered a disastrous car accident earlier in the year, followed by six months in hospital. Yet her attitude remained positive.

When I mentioned the accident, she said, 'I lived, didn't I?' As always, her thinking was clear and honest. 'God was watching over me. By all rights I should have died. But here I am.'

'I'm glad,' I told her. I was filled with happiness as we talked together, the wind from the river blowing away all confusion within. We both knew something special had happened, some line had been crossed; but Ceil finally said, 'I can't see you any more, you know. You're a married man.'

*Not really.*

'I wouldn't feel right, seeing a married man.'

'OK then.' I squeezed her hand. 'But let's not leave here for a few minutes.'

She nodded, smiled and kissed me.

The hits continued: 'Poor Little Rich Girl' for Steve, 'Don't Try to Fight It, Baby' for Edyie, a duet for both of them, 'I Can't Stop Talking About You'.

With so much chart action, it was a perfect time to strike out on my own and start a production company. It was also time to embark on a new and separate life. Felicia and I had tried our best to move closer, without success. I packed and drove away in the spring of 1963.

Our final clash took place at Associated Studios on West Seventh Avenue. I was doing a few sides with myself as the artist—songs written by Bacharach and David. I still wanted that elusive hit as a singer.

Charlie Calello, responsible for orchestrating the Four Seasons' records, was doing my arrangements.

I was in the middle of a take when I noticed Felicia walk into the control booth. I missed a note and did it again. No luck. The next take was even worse.

Felicia waved at me. I couldn't go on until I had found out what she wanted.

What she wanted was a reconciliation. 'You've got to come back,' she insisted. 'You've got to. You don't answer your phone. . . you won't take my calls. You can't treat me this way.'

Why, I wondered, was she so anxious to hang on to something we both knew was a terrible mistake? Pride? A sense of failure?

# 7
## *Please, God, Let Me Sleep*

'We don't love each other,' I wanted to say. 'We never did.'

I pulled her into a small office packed with crates and boxes of tape. 'I demand that you come back,' Felicia said.

The word 'demand' gave me the strength to stand firm. 'No.' Suddenly she slapped me.

I stumbled backwards, upsetting a row of boxes. Several of them flew off the shelves. Boxes opened and tape unravelled at our feet. Charlie dashed in, followed by one of the secretaries.

'Everything OK?' the secretary asked.

Neither of us spoke. Felicia stared at me, as if to say: 'All right, that's enough. Now come home with me.'

She knew how much I wanted peace; how much I strained to 'be nice'. I didn't move.

'Hey, man, we'd better get back inside,' Charlie said. 'I've got to let the band go in twenty minutes.'

Felicia stared rigidly as I began to follow him.

'You haven't heard the last of this,' she threatened, edging towards the exit. 'You'll be sorry. I'll make you sorry. I swear it.' I felt sweat trickling from under my arms, even though the studio was ice cold from air conditioning.

'Man, you should have let her have it,' said Gary, the engineer. 'If it was me, I'd have killed her.'

I knew Gary was all talk, but I had my father's crazy Polish temper. It was a part of me I rejected—a part I associated with everything animal and low-class. But it was there.

I managed a feeble, 'It doesn't matter,' but my throat closed, strangling off the words. I mumbled an excuse and headed for the men's toilets. They were empty. I turned on the cold water and splashed it against my face. The water spurted loudly from the tap, but it was drowned out by my crashing heartbeat. The walls began to contract; my vision blurred. The echo of my screams nearly exploded my skull, caged and desperate, though I knew no sound was coming from my lips. I had to control the panic, control the senseless, hammering demons that were taking possession of my body and brain.

Finally the shattering heartbeats calmed, and there was an eerie, unnatural quiet, broken only by running water. I groped for the sink and turned the tap off, grateful to be alive.

During 1964 my dependence on diet pills increased. My weight continued to fluctuate, dropping dramatically, then bursting back up. At night I relied on Valium to soothe the hyperactivity the diet pills caused. Insomnia, always bad, continued to plague me. My mind chugged through the long hours between midnight and morning: 'I've got to make it big. I've got to get over the top. If I just make it, I can sleep. Please, God, let me sleep.'

I increased the dosage from thirty to forty milligrams, and soon that wasn't enough.

I *had* to sleep, because if I didn't I couldn't maintain my non-stop working regime. I couldn't satisfy the never-ending, now-internalised demands of Rose Kasha.

*Don't worry*, I reassured myself. *Everybody I know is on diet pills. Everyone I know takes Valium. They're harmless.* An actor I knew observed, 'Look, it's practically a status symbol. What red-blooded guy doesn't take something?'

My most creative experience during this time centred around Rodney Dangerfield. I first became aware of

Rodney through my friend Herb Gluck. Herb had seen Rodney in the Catskill Mountains and felt he had untapped ability.

I respected Herb's judgement. As proved later by his best-selling biography, *The Mick*, Herb had an innate understanding of talent. He urged me to come to the mountains and check Rodney out.

When Rodney and I met, he admitted, 'I've worked in clubs so bad you took two steps down, socially and economically.' But I saw the unmined abilities Herb had referred to and suggested he concentrate on his loser image, rather than bombarding audiences with unrelated jokes. I persuaded a good friend, Irving Mansfield, to put Rodney on TV. Irving was the producer of a popular variety show, *On Broadway Tonight*, and he agreed with me about Rodney's potential.

I produced Rodney's first album, 'The Loser', which became a cult item and started him towards his *No Respect* image. I was delighted when the world recognised his genius and made him a superstar.

Irving remained a key figure in my life. He became my adviser, my guide, my father, in a way my real father had never been. I liked his dapper, Goddard Lieberson style, his blue cashmere jackets and red silk handkerchiefs. And I liked his personal style too: kind and gentle, yet intense and high-powered. After years of success as press agent for Milton Berle, Eddie Cantor and Billy Rose, then as producer of the *Arthur Godfrey Show*, Irving was devoting all his considerable energy to the promotion of his wife, Jacqueline Susann's, literary career.

Their mutual affection and teamwork were an inspiration. Growing up, I had only witnessed two people pulling apart, clashing on all major issues. My brief and painful marriage to Felicia was over by 1964; we were divorced. Irving and Jackie, on the other hand, fulfilled their dreams through each other. Jackie's first book, *Every Night*

*Josephine* (about her pet poodle), was gaining popularity. I liked the title and suggested a song be written around it. Irving was enthusiastic. The record was released soon after and helped accelerate the book's sales.

*Every Night Josephine* eventually hit the Top 10 non-fiction list in *Time* magazine, a tribute to Jackie's talent and Irving's tenacity. *Valley of the Dolls* followed shortly after.

Irving and Jackie were generous and caring; they adopted me, treated me like a son. Most accounts of Irving and Jackie stress their genius at promotion, but these anecdotes leave out their dedication and hard work. Jackie took her writing seriously. She knew the world of entertainment from the inside, as model and actress, and wanted the Hollywood scene portrayed with honesty. She hated the way Hollywood was caricatured in second-rate novels.

'These people have been through the mill,' she told me. 'It's not all glamour. They hurt, they have fears, they live with constant insecurity. It's that side of the famous that I want to put into print.'

When she talked about the secret agonies of celebrities, she was talking about her own private battle with cancer, although I didn't know it then.

Irving treated me to lunch at least twice a week at the Oak Room in the Plaza, filling my ears with show business vignettes and sound advice. One of his lessons was: 'There isn't *anyone* you can't meet. Don't take the direct route, like asking for a job. You'll never get one that way. Think to yourself, "Who is this man's barber? His dentist?" Barbers and dentists talk a lot. Surround the troops!'

These statements were similar to the suggestions Mickey Rooney offered when I worked with him on *Pete's Dragon* in 1976. 'If you can't get in through the front door, try the back door. If that's locked, climb in through the window. If you can't squeeze through the window, try the roof.'

In 1965 Harriet Wasser, the high-powered publicity

agent who had helped promote Bobby Darin to success, introduced me to a tall, lanky songwriter named Joel Hirschhorn. Joel had been signed to RCA as a recording artist. The company dubbed him Hathaway, for reasons he could never figure out, and sent him on tour with dark glasses and a crew cut. Hathaway made a mild chart showing, but Joel decided to concentrate on just writing after his deal ended. The result was 'All About Love', cut by rhythm and blues great Clyde McPhatter. To support himself, Joel became a court reporter, as well as a pianist at weekends with his rock band 'The Blazers'.

We had natural chemistry, an interlocking of needs and ambitions. Two kids from the Bronx and Brooklyn, we both had tastes ranging from Chuck Berry to Frank Sinatra.

This need to hear and try everything was a common bond. We wanted to write for records, films, theatre, TV— and we had the youthful energy and versatility to accomplish it.

I remember talking over a cup of coffee at the Pink Cloud, a diner on Columbus Avenue in Manhattan. Joel and I liked the Pink Cloud because it had a greasy, comfortably chaotic feel. It also had a jukebox that contained a complete collection of Motown hits, from early Smokey Robinson and the Miracles to Diana Ross' 'You Can't Hurry Love'.

He listened, blue eyes thoughtful and attentive, as I babbled wildly on. 'We can be Richard Rodgers. We can be Leiber and Stoller. We can be Bacharach and David. We can be Holland, Dozier and Holland. . . we can be *more famous than they are.*'

Despite a history as piano prodigy and student at the High School of Performing Arts, Joel wanted rock and roll as much as I did. He still lived at home with his parents, but was ready to make his move.

From the start we were friends. Best friends. I'd start a

sentence, Joel would finish it. If I had an idea for a tune, he'd sing the following line, and it would be exactly what I had heard. We were completely of one mind.

We were also alike in our need for harmony. In working together, if Joel said, 'I think your melody is pretty good,' it meant he hated it. If I asked him to 'file something away for a future time', it meant that the lyric or tune in question should be immediately discarded. We instinctively grasped this language, the language of let's-never-argue, let's-not-hurt-the-other's-feelings.

Joel typed 120 words a minute, a skill acquired from his court stenography days. Sometimes I would come up with a lyric line, then turn and start to repeat it. 'I've already got it down,' was his invariable comment. I used to wonder how the typewriter didn't start smoking or simply explode. This spectacular ability helped our writing pace and rhythm. Occasionally stenography proved a draw-back. In Joel's dedication to speed, he would write down a lyric we had just completed—in shorthand. If I wanted to examine the lyric alone at the end of the day, I'd pick it up and find our afternoon's work in code. Part of our work procedure was to assemble a list of possible titles. They too were frequently a mass of lines and curlicues when I wanted to go over them.

'*Please* stick to English,' I begged. With a grin he promised to comply. Most of the time he did.

The songs poured out at an astonishing rate. We wrote compulsively, day and night, gathering titles, scribbling bits of tunes on napkins, shopping bags, stationery, what-ever was handy. I carried a title book everywhere. We combed the music trades, *Billboard*, *Cashbox* and *Record World*, to see who was popular, who needed material. No piano was safe, whether it be in a hotel lobby, a restaurant or a music shop. Joel's piano bench bulged with lead sheets and as our file of demo records grew it threatened to take over the room.

We sat in cinemas writing lyrics on our laps, undeterred by the dark. People ordered us to shut up, distracted by our steady stream of dialogue... 'How about this bridge?'...'Let's change the first line to...' 'Say, the tune should go mmm mmmm mmmm...'

Cars shrieked to a stop when we crossed 8th Avenue or Columbus; we were too immersed in the creative process to see them. And we never slept. If either of us had an idea at four in the morning, we'd reach for the phone. Whenever an opening presented itself, we aimed for it. We lived in studios—Associated, Duchess and Pincus kept us going. I learned a valuable lesson. The brain rises to meet any challenge if pushed. Logic told us that five, six songs a week was an unrealistic, absurd goal. But need, ambition, obsession, youthful hunger made these five songs possible. We were too naïve, too ignorant, to recognise it couldn't be done—so we did it!

'Let's try for Elvis Presley,' I suggested one morning at the Pink Cloud.

'Elvis? That's crazy. Leiber and Stoller have him all locked up.'

'Not any more. We can get him.'

We submitted a dozen songs to his publishing representative, Freddie Bienstock, of Hill and Range Music. Freddie subsidised demo after demo.

Nothing happened.

We weren't discouraged. Elvis was the Number One film star, and we wanted to open the door to films. Films meant the possibility of one day winning an Oscar.

The word 'Oscar' had a profound effect on Joel. Any mention of films sparked him; he loved films with a passion. He was one of those buffs who could recite all the lines from *Double Indemnity*, or sing obscure numbers like 'I think I'm gonna like it here' from Elvis Presley's *Fun in Acapulco*. When we weren't together, he lived in cinemas. One of his dreams was to be a film critic, and he often wrote reviews for relaxation.

Joel had a few odd quirks: as a former court stenographer, he was accustomed to writing down speech; and he would scribble conversations in the air or under the table as they flowed. After taking imaginary notes, he would erase them with the flick of his palm.

Joel's love of films was matched by my worship of songwriters. I concocted pet theories:

(a) Irving Berlin writes like a Jewish grandmother; he asks and answers a question. *Maybe It's Because I Love You so Much, Maybe That's Why You Love Me so Little; They Say That Falling in Love Is Wonderful, It's Wonderful, so They Say; How Much Do I Love You, I'll Tell You no Lie, How Deep Is the Ocean, How High Is the Sky?*

(b) Oscar Hammerstein is always indirect; he can't come out and say 'I love you'; *People Will Say We're in Love; Do I Love You Because You're Beautiful or Are You Beautiful Because I Love You?*

As a result, I was able to project into the minds and feelings of artists. Joel had the same facility, and the artists who did our material ranged from Peggy Lee to Anthony Newley, Jackie Wilson to Fred Astaire.

'Look at this!' Joel shouted. We were once again in the Pink Cloud—we practically lived there during the 1960s. The Pink Cloud, with its underdone omelettes, watery orange juice and bitter coffee, had evolved into a symbol of all our struggles. Its shoddiness was romantic.

'What's the matter?'

Joel thrust a copy of the current *Cashbox* into my hands, and I stared at a full page ad on page 28. Neither of us ever forgot the page number. 'Your Time Hasn't Come Yet, Baby'—the new Elvis Presley single by Kasha and Hirschhorn.

We were overcome. It's one thing to take a confident approach; another to see a dream realised.

# 8

## *Starting Again*

*Run faster. You've made some inroads. Press on and make the best of them.*

In 1968, I flew to Hollywood to consult with Liberty Records about producing Nancy Ames. While there, I went to the *Speedway* set for the last days of shooting and met Elvis. He only reinforced what Jacqueline Susann had said about the insecurities of celebrities. At first he appeared relaxed, joking with people. When I got him alone for a few minutes, though, he was quiet and withdrawn; he seemed frightened, totally opposite from the King image I had read about so often.

'It's not a great picture,' he remarked, almost apologetically. That line offered me a clue: Elvis wanted to do better things than the mediocre Hollywood vehicles he had committed himself to. But by 1968, he had become too much a victim of big money and merchandising to dig his way out.

My own panic was increasing. Palpitations, butterflies in my stomach, a sense of jeopardy—all became daily companions, even though I was still able to conceal them from Joel.

I started watching for similar symptoms in other people. Soon I developed an intuitive awareness of phobics around me. I'd catch a pair of frightened eyes in a lift, or notice an elderly woman tremble when requested to sign a cheque at the bank. Nervous illness was everywhere.

On a flight to San Francisco, I sat next to a redheaded woman in her thirties who kept fastening and unfastening her seat belt. She grasped my arm more and more tightly as we talked.

'Somebody's got to let me off this plane,' she whispered. At the time we were 31,000 ft above San Jose.

'You'll be all right,' I assured her; but she wasn't. She repeated, 'Get me off this plane,' spreading concern and fear with brushfire rapidity throughout the aircraft. Stewardesses rushed over and led her to the rear of the plane, unsuccessfully attempting to soothe her mounting hysteria. I never released my terrors publicly, the way this woman did. I had to appear brave. But self-imposed isolation left me desperately lonely. Fellowship with other people is vital if you're to become desensitised, freed of phobic symptoms; and I held all my emotions in. I felt increasingly adrift, without a sense of belonging.

The times didn't help either. The year 1967 was an alarming period for all freelance composers. I watched helplessly as the Brill Building era died. With the arrival of the Beatles (already hailed by the London *Times* as 'the greatest composers since Beethoven'), singer–songwriters seized power; and the charts bulged with groups from England as well as America: The Rolling Stones, The Kinks, The Animals, Simon and Garfunkel, The Beach Boys. None of them considered doing 'outside' songs, and before long *Billboard*'s Top 100 listed fewer than fifteen artists who welcomed tunes from a freelancer.

It was a period of panic. Neil Sedaka was suddenly derailed. There was a pained, what-can-I-do-now? expression on the faces of Gerry Goffin and Carole King. For Carole the late 1960s was a period of searching, of struggling to become an artist; a struggle brilliantly consummated with the popularity of 'Tapestry'.

Morty Schuman (co-writer, with Doc Pomus, of many Elvis Presley hits as well as 'Save the Last Dance for Me') went abroad and became a cabaret star in *Jacques Brel Is Alive and Well and Living in Paris*. Burt Bacharach left for Hollywood and continued his string of hits with Hal David by writing movie themes.

I chose the Bacharach route. Burt and I were friends, and he made the motion picture world seem excitingly attainable. Joel and I scored a film about ghetto life, *The Unemployables*. We also wrote a rock score for an excruciating, low-budget venture entitled *The Fat Spy*, starring Jayne Mansfield.

Jayne had climbed to success on her curves, but she took herself seriously as an 'actress'. We wrote a few far-from-immortal lyrics for her:

> I'd like to be a rose in your garden
> But I'm just a thorn in your side.

Jayne rehearsed the words hundreds of times, straining to extract their 'deeper' meanings. Joel and I sat in the record booth with her when she did the session, watching her grimace dramatically, as though every word was being torn from her soul.

Life was no rose garden, but it had its humorous aspects, even concerning my family. I was living with a Catholic girl named Emily. I knew my parents would disapprove, so I told them Joel and I were living together. When my mother called Joel's flat, which she did frequently, I was never there. Joel had an automatic response: 'Al's shopping, Mrs Kasha.'

'You're always shopping,' she told me indignantly. 'What's wrong with Joel's feet? Doesn't *he* ever go to the shops?'

'Shopping's my job,' I explained. 'Joel does the dishes.'

The situation reached its ludicrous height in 1967 when the New York blackout spread darkness all over Manhattan. My mother called and Joel, disorientated by the circumstances, answered in robot fashion: 'He's out shopping.'

'Shopping? During the blackout? I don't believe it.'

'We . . . needed a few groceries.'

'He must be there. Put him on the phone.'

'I swear, he's at the market. He'll be back soon.'

Joel contacted me and I called her back. She told me I was being used, that Joel was a selfish monster, and I should get another flatmate willing to carry his share of the load.

Then the guilt was poured on: 'Larry calls me. Why don't you?'

'I called you on Wednesday.'

'So? This is Friday. And I thought you were calling me at eight Wednesday. You didn't call till ten.'

Her intervention on my behalf was sometimes embarrassing. In 1967, Larry directed a revival of *Showboat* at Lincoln Center, an occasion that reintroduced me to my childhood idol, Richard Rodgers. Rodgers was co-producer of the revival. My mother noticed him in the lobby and said, 'Now *there's* a success. That's what you have to be.' Then she raced to his side and reminded him who I was. 'The boy who played Little Jake in *Annie Get Your Gun*,' she said, as he smiled politely.

'You write for the theatre, don't you darling?'

He nodded.

'Well,' my mother burst out, thinking of my song in *Speedway*, 'my son Alfred is a songwriter too. Only he writes for *movies*.'

I cringed. Here was the greatest show writer of his time, perhaps in history, regarded as an equal with the man who had written a tune for Elvis Presley's *Speedway*.

Rodgers had also written for 'movies'. That year his *Sound of Music* had become the biggest box office film of all time.

'You could team up with Alfred . . . now that Oscar is dead,' my mother suggested.

'Mum, *please.*'

'Why not? Maybe Mr Rodgers needs a new partner.'

Needless to say, the team of Rodgers and Kasha never materialised.

Those Broadway opening nights my mother had dreamed about were now realities, and she relished every minute of them. When photographers took pictures back-stage, her mink stole was more prominent than the images of the stars. Only on these occasions did she wear her mink, and acquaintances on Avenue M never saw it. Convinced that the neighbours would wish her ill and give her the evil eye, she wrapped the mink in a white sheet and stuffed it into a suitcase. Then, on a dark street several miles away, she would switch outfits and prepare herself for the big evening ahead.

Larry earned most of her approval as the years passed. He was more attentive. Despite my childhood promise to give her a mink, Larry had beaten me to it. He took her out with his friends and saw to it that she occupied front row centre when she attended a show—his or anyone else's. He remained a bachelor, while I committed the cardinal sin of getting married. Even though she still claimed, 'Larry is my right eye and you're my left eye;' even though she still sang 'You'll Never Know Just How Much I Love You' when she hugged me, her Lawrence was Number One man in her heart. My father knew, and increasingly resented, his position as Number Three. The calls from my mother about him became more frequent: 'He beat me last night. . . he's ruining my life. . . I need my sons.'

'Mum, you've got to move out. Get your own place. I'll pay for it.'

'No, darling. When you make it . . . when you can afford it . . . then . . .'

'I'm doing fine. I can afford it.'

'Not yet, darling. Soon. When it's time.' There was a pause.

'Maybe I could live with you or Larry.'

'That's not a good idea, Mum.'

'I wouldn't be in the way. I promise.'

I ignored her plea. I think she knew I would refuse. She wasn't quite ready to make the final break from Avenue M.

Joel and I kept writing as 1968 melted into 1969. Hippies with beads, reeking of marijuana, filled the streets and I grew more and more restless with New York. I dreamed of living in California or Nashville or even London—anywhere but Manhattan where my parents could, if they chose, jump on the subway and reach me within half an hour.

My moods became more erratic, owing to the diet pills I took to suppress my appetite and the downers I took to mellow me out. Joel bore the brunt of my unpredictable personality swings.

At that crucial moment, February 1968, I received a call from the publishing wing of CBS, April Blackwood. Would I consider running the firm in Los Angeles?

The answer was 'yes', even before I heard any talk of salary. Working in LA would place me in the thick of the motion picture industry.

Events sped forward, like film being wound ahead at twice the normal speed. Ceil called. It had been four years since my divorce. We met again and I knew, intuitively, that this was it. If any woman could share my life, understand my workaholism, lend support, Ceil was the one. She understood the music profession, knew its pressures and demands.

I thought of that night by the East River, the warming sound of her laugh, the playfulness of her humour, the beauty of her spirit. I thought of those hours when, briefly, I had felt calm and unafraid.

Ceil decided to convert to Judaism. She wanted a united feeling in our home; a sharing of roots and faith. She wanted our children to grow up without confusion and conflicting loyalties.

As I had expected, my parents were passionately opposed to my marriage; opposed to Ceil on principle as a *shiksa* (her conversion didn't count), and opposed to my planned move to California. When Ceil and I went to Avenue M for dinner, my mother would talk *about* her, never to her: 'See what *she* wants . . . . Give her more potatoes . . . . Pass her the roast.'

'My name isn't "her",' Ceil said, hurt by the rejection.

'Maybe if you were marrying a Jewish girl . . . .'

'I did marry one,' I reminded her.

After the conversion, Ceil, my mother and I went for breakfast, and Ceil unwittingly ordered bacon and eggs. My mother straightened up, squared her mink-padded shoulders and said, 'She'll never be a Jew.'

The incident made me recall Larry's brief engagement. I had liked his fiancée, a tall, attractive brunette named Peggy. 'She says she's thirty,' my mother remarked. 'I think closer to thirty-five. Look around the eyes. And why hasn't she ever been married? There's something wrong.'

Or: 'Maybe she has been married, and she's hiding it. I don't trust her.'

Or: 'Did she go to college? I don't think she went to college. She's not smart enough for Larry.'

Then, running out of reasons: 'I know. . . my heart tells me. . . that it's wrong, wrong, wrong.'

A few weeks later, Larry broke his engagement.

Now it was my turn, and I had no intention of letting her destroy a relationship that meant so much to me.

Ceil's parents, by contrast, welcomed me immediately as a son. Her mother called me a 'prince', and told Ceil, 'Be good to him.' Her father said something even more meaningful: 'You're my son. I know you're Jewish, but listen, after all. . . Jesus was a Jew.'

# 9

## *Hollywood Lifeline*

California was perfect through the autumn of 1968. Ceil and I rented a beautiful home in North Hollywood, complete with spacious garden and pool—a far cry from living over a shop. We loved the weather and the natural beauty of the countryside. Talk of a giant earthquake that would sweep California into the sea was rampant that year, but we laughed it off.

Joel decided to share a house on Laurel Canyon with our mutual friend, songwriter Gerry Robinson. We were set to write lyrics to Marvin Hamlisch's melodies for *The April Fools*, a film starring Jack Lemmon. And Ceil was pregnant.

*I have it all*, I thought, as the American Airlines jumbo jet roared through the clouds from LA to New York. Seated to the right and left of me were two top CBS executives, one president of the picture division. Joel and I had three records in the charts simultaneously: 'Will You Be Staying After Sunday?' and 'Don't Wake Me Up in the Morning, Michael' (both by the Peppermint Rainbow) and 'Stay and Love Me All Summer' by Brian Hyland.

'Thank you, God, for all these blessings,' I whispered, just before the terror began.

'You all right?' one of my companions asked. I nodded, sweat streaming down my forehead. I excused myself and stumbled to the toilets. This time it wasn't only palpitations. I felt trapped. The walls of the tiny cubicle intensified my fear. I was sealed inside my father's wardrobe again, and this time it was suspended in mid air. The prospect of walking back to my seat, negotiating the narrow aisle, was worse.

I felt faint; my head was whirling. All sense of time and place deserted me. Voices faded in and out.

*You're an important executive*, I reminded myself. *The head of a major publishing operation. Yesterday you spoke to CBS record company president Clive Davis. This morning you met with Jack Lemmon. Get a hold of yourself.*

Somehow I did, after dousing my face with cold water and holding my breath for half a minute. The panic subsided, and I returned to my seat, falling normally into a discussion about the state of the record business and what influence San Francisco and the psychedelic scene would exert on the industry in years to come.

I flew many other times in 1968 and 1969 without fear. Eventually I persuaded myself that the attack was an isolated incident. Yet a part of my brain kept waiting, like an animal in the jungle, every nerve sensitised to a future threat.

Creatively, the late 1960s were an exciting, fruitful period. Joel, Marvin and I wrote 'Wake Up' for *The April Fools*. The Chambers Brothers cut it and a hit single emerged. We had an opportunity to collaborate with that master of urban blues, Taj Mahal. Our song 'Give Your Woman What She Wants' also appeared in the film.

In 1970, I heard through the executive grapevine that Sal Ianucci of National General was searching for someone to head the company's new record division. The announcement had little effect, until they contacted me and asked if I would consider the job.

Two thoughts assailed me at the same time: *What an honour* and *Don't take it!*

I was a songwriter first. Would this deeper immersion into the executive world pull me further away from my first love? Could I be executive by day and songwriter by night?

Ceil was doubtful. 'You know what a workaholic you are,' she said. 'You always give everything 100 per cent. If you carry two separate careers at once, you'll crack up.'

'Not if I divide my time properly.'

'The two jobs will overlap. They have to. You know this business. And when will you have time to sleep?'

*It doesn't matter. I never sleep anyway.*

'I love you,' Ceil said, burying her head in my shoulder. 'I want you alive and healthy at forty.'

The birth of our daughter Dana decided me. Golden-haired, blue-eyed Dana was the greatest gift in a life already showered with blessings. From birth she displayed the sweetest disposition, the brightest smile, the most giving nature of anyone, child or adult, I had ever known.

She would have the best, no matter what I had to do to get it for her. So would Ceil, who had been born on Gunhill Road in the Bronx, and had experienced the same economic deprivation I had. I wanted their lot to be an easy one.

Becoming President of a record company added more to my prestige than to my peace of mind. The corporate game, even under the best of circumstances, requires a certain paranoia. Executives must protect themselves from the competitive danger of rivals who need to discredit the next man to build up their own positions.

Another emotional split occurred. Not only did I have to divide myself between songwriter and executive, I was compulsively driven to maintain two mind-sets within the executive framework: the get-them-or-they'll-get-me mentality and the 'be nice' syndrome—directly contradictory goals. Powerful executives are rarely concerned with being 'nice', nor do they care about satisfying Rose Kasha's requirement, 'Do they like you?' Fair means or foul, they aim to get ahead.

Work wasn't enough. In Hollywood, giving parties for the 'right people' was stressed to me by Dolly Parton's manager, Sandy Gallin. Sandy advised, 'Hollywood's a town built on publicity, on hype. Hire a press agent. Buy a home in Beverly Hills. And get yourself invited to as many important functions as you can.'

Ceil was a natural hostess; she was gregarious and loved people. So we threw a surprise birthday party for Lionel Newman, head of music at Twentieth Century Fox, and did the same shortly after for E. Y. (Yip) Harburg, lyricist for *The Wizard of Oz* and *Finian's Rainbow*. Yip was particularly important to us, as friend and teacher. He had encouraged our theatrical ambitions in New York, analysing our work and helping us polish our writing skills.

For Yip's party we invited composer Jerry Herman, a boyhood friend of mine, Alexis Smith, Craig Stevens, Gary Collins, Mary Ann Mobley and Michele Lee, just a few of the talented guests who admired his work. A high spot of the night was Yip singing his own classic 'Somewhere Over the Rainbow'.

These events were always lively and tuneful. But there was pressure too. I was nervous beforehand, wondering how to please the stars who attended. I geared myself up, along with Joel, to perform our songs, hoping for a favourable response, and breathing a sigh of relief when I got one. And the typical Hollywood conversations that emphasised 'What are you doing?' rather than 'Who are you?' wore me down.

After a long time, I discovered that parties weren't what counted; only the quality of the work.

It was enjoyable and challenging to strive for quality on our next project, *The Cheyenne Social Club*. Gene Kelly, the director, provided creative stimulus, and the stars we were to compose a duet for, James Stewart and Henry Fonda, were legends and personal favourites.

Joel and I felt awe in the presence of Kelly, Stewart and Fonda. What impressed us most, beyond the individuality they projected, was their truth. They knew who they were, and never tampered with their natural personalities. I observed Fonda's professionalism when National General, producers of *The Cheyenne Social Club*, asked me to cut 300 spots of Fonda plugging our song, 'Rolling Stone'. He was on location in Oregon, filming *Sometimes a Great Notion* with Paul Newman, and I found him in a small hotel.

Fonda was less intimidating in jeans and red plaid shirt. My engineer and I set up. With complete ease, Fonda lay in bed, repeating phrases: 'Hello, Kansas. My friend Jimmy Stewart and I have a new record, 'Rolling Stone'. Hope you'll put us on your playlist . . . . Hello, Akron . . . . Hello, San Diego. . . .'

After 150 were done, I was hesitant about asking for more. Fonda spotted a stack of papers in my briefcase, listing the stations that wanted spots. 'How many more do you need?' he asked.

'Uh. . . about 150.'

Without missing a beat he said, 'Well, let's do 'em then. Wanna give the song all the promotion we can.'

Fonda's handling of the situation was the most impressive definition of 'being a pro' that I had ever witnessed. No fuss, no temperament, no patronising airs—just do the job, help the picture, play on the team.

Gene gave me more than a lesson on professionalism; he heightened my desire to do large-scale, ambitious things—a full film musical like *Singing in the Rain*, or a Broadway show. He was warm and likable and encouraged my dreams.

He also taught me a valuable, if painful, lesson. Until 1970, I had always been chronically late—a childish gambit to get attention. One night I had an appointment with Gene at his home on Rodeo Drive. I don't recall what delayed me, but I presented myself on his doorstep at nine for an eight o'clock get-together.

Gene's normally amiable, grinning face was purple with rage when I arrived. 'I've never been treated so rudely,' he said. 'There's no excuse for keeping someone waiting this long.' With that he marched up the stairs and left me alone, completely humiliated.

He was right, of course. And from that day forward I was never late again. When I saw Gene next, he made no reference to the incident; he was as sweet and caring as ever. Joel and I loved to listen to him talk. He brought the MGM days glitteringly alive, referring to that constant state of anticipation and joy that he, Judy Garland, Fred Astaire and all the writers and musicians felt when making a film. 'It was never work,' he said. 'We beat our brains out, but somehow it was fun.' He also told us how the studio had said, 'You'll never make it with the name Gene Kelly. Change it to Gene Black because you have black hair.' He chuckled. 'Can you imagine Garland and Black? What a disaster.'

Most of all, Gene projected a love of work—the kind of love that once prompted Picasso to remark, 'Always you put more of yourself into your work until one day—you never know exactly which day—you *are* your work. Your work in life is the ultimate seduction.'

Writing had become, by then, my ultimate seduction, and I felt increasingly torn by the executive responsibilities that wrenched me from it. As Ceil had predicted, Joel and I worked late into the night. I had to triple and quadruple my Valium dosages to calm down and grab any sleep at all. I was in a stupor through breakfast; rarely could I string together a cohesive sentence.

Gene adored every aspect of his career, but he didn't suffer as I did. He wanted to do his best, but not to say, 'See, I did it.' A job well done appeared to be sufficient reward.

He wanted to achieve—not for Mum and Dad, not for

old schoolteachers who had slighted him, but for himself.

Joel got married in April 1969. On the surface it seemed as though he and his wife Jill belonged in two separate worlds. Joel was the New York boy who identified with Woody Allen. Jill was the daredevil West Hartford WASP; one who had made the perilous 136-foot dive from the Acapulco cliffs.

But they had music in common. Jill was a gifted song-writer, intensely driven, determined to show the world she could make an important mark in her profession.

It was a loving bond, but the competitive element caused problems. Both kept busy—Jill with an album on RCA Victor, for which she sang and wrote all the material; Joel with our joint films and hit records. The competition was sticky but manageable. More seriously, Jill felt Joel was putting too much time and effort into our work, rather than spending weekends and evenings at home with her.

'She doesn't want me to be a workaholic,' Joel would explain. Intellectually I understood. Jill was the child of an alcoholic herself; her mother had died of the disease and like all adult children of alcoholics, she needed a tremen-dous amount of love and reassurance. The only trouble was, her needs clashed with my goals, my timetable. I had my own race to run, my mother to please, my peers to impress. Joel and I, as partners, had to work towards those objectives. He had to be available night and day when key assignments came in, and I felt that Jill, as a fellow song-writer, should understand the erratic, unpredictable dead-lines of show business.

Joel and Jill solved—or at least handled—their conflicts in a strange fashion. Jill was a borderline anorexic. She ate only one meal a day and lived in a state of semi-starvation. Joel loved chocolate and sweets. He began to overeat, to consume huge portions of cake, ice cream and sweets. It was a game at first. They would laugh as he finished off packets of biscuits. They joked about his Jewish appetite, his love of delicatessens. But the pounds piled on. His sweet tooth vicariously satisfied her unfulfilled longings for meals of her own.

It was almost as though he were saying, 'I'll eat for you if you'll let me have the time I want to work.'

This unspoken deal between them preserved the balance enough to keep our partnership functioning. Joel's weight, meanwhile, continued to rise. He was caught in the middle of two powerful forces. Jill pulled one way, I pulled the other; and he, as a lifelong peacemaker, sought to satisfy both of us. His attempt to be the perfect partner and the perfect husband resulted in high blood pressure.

He ignored the doctor's warnings, as their game slipped slowly out of control. Our work, miraculously, got done. All this juggling resulted in a steady flow of successful songs.

My executive juggling resulted in a $4 million tape deal for National General with Ampex, to be distributed through Buddah Records. It was the largest tape deal ever made up to that time, 1970, and a strong way to establish my effectiveness. For the moment, I enjoyed the privileges heaped on a division president: limousines, private jets, a floor-long suite at the Waldorf Astoria where Cole Porter had once lived, trips to Cannes, Spain, London. No longer was I trapped above a shop in Brooklyn.

Except inside: my emotions lingered back there. I struggled to escape that prison, not knowing my sentence had been commuted. I felt like a rejected ten-year-old when the National General bigwigs didn't acknowledge my achievement. What I didn't realise was the major trouble National General's motion picture division was in. They needed much more than $4 million to offset a series of box office disappointments.

I encountered heavy anti-rock-'n'-roll sentiment. One of my primary jobs was to recommend writers for National General films. After suggesting Brill Building great Gerry

Goffin (ex-husband of Carole King, a gigantic record seller and a superlative lyricist), a director stared coldly and said, 'We don't want rock 'n' roll writers. That music is for kids. It's rubbish.' It was bewildering. The Beatles had already made legendary contributions to music, eliciting praise from establishment heroes like Leonard Bernstein. Songs about protest and civil rights and flower power had shaken the world. Dylan had denounced 'The Masters of War'; Barry McGuire had warned about 'The Eve of Destruction'; Joni Mitchell had evoked the beauty and significance of 'Woodstock'.

And here was a director saying, 'Rock 'n' roll is for kids.' I knew it was only a matter of time before films caught up, embraced rock and responded to its creative and financial implications. But the era of sound track fever was still years away. The 1994 Oscars, which included five rock hits in their Best Song category, were in the undreamed-of future.

# 10

# *Panic*

Maintaining a full-time writing and executive schedule was becoming unbearable. I walked around with a permanent headache. My insomnia was worse than ever, and I piled another crushing pressure on top of all the others. In addition to pop song writing and executive responsibility, I now plunged into the task of creating a Broadway show.

My longing for Broadway was stronger than ever, due to a recent collaboration with Charles Aznavour. Joel and I had written English lyrics to several of Charles' songs, including 'Like Roses' and 'Little Fool, I Love You', and Charles had performed them all in his Broadway fledged theatre vehicle of our own. The project we selected—because it was family-orientated and in the public domain—was Charles Dickens' *David Copperfield*.

We read the book aloud and picked parts we felt were appropriate for songs. After completing five, we contacted Gene Kelly about the possibility of directing.

'Sounds like a great idea,' said Gene. 'Come over tonight and play the stuff for me.'

When I hung up the phone I was trembling. Presenting our material to Gene meant everything to me. I had always considered myself a show writer, deep down. Rodgers and Hammerstein were still the two men I wanted us to emulate. If Gene, a man of vast theatrical experience, an actor who had worked with Rodgers and Hart on *Pal Joey* and Cole Porter on *The Pirate*—if *he* liked it, it meant we were fit to function in that rarefied world.

By sheer coincidence, a leading London producer, Sir Bernard Delfont, was staying at the Beverly Hills Hotel, and Gene invited him to hear the music.

Joel and I each took a pep pill beforehand (Ritalin) to ensure an energetic, show-stopping performance. Ritalin was the latest of my uppers; I found it cleared the brain and enabled us to get more work done. Ritalin seemed harmless. It wasn't really a powerful stimulant, I told myself. After all, doctors gave it to hyperactive children to slow them down, though it had the reverse effect on adults. If a five-year-old could take it without harm, surely it couldn't threaten two healthy men in their thirties.

I also felt, as many drug-dependent people do, that I had a high tolerance for pills. Valium and Eskatrol hardly affected me. I only turned to Ritalin under special, stressful conditions.

Joel and I didn't simply perform the score that night—we lived it. I was David Copperfield, Aunt Betsy Trotwood and Mr Murdstone rolled into one; Joel was Uriah Heep, Mr Micawber and Mr Dick. I became, once again, the kid from Rose and Irving's barber shop, singing myself hoarse for approval. Joel pounded the piano until the keys nearly collapsed. Gene grinned more and more at the conclusion of each number, particularly 'Something Will Turn Up', an ode to optimism sung by Wilkins Micawber.

'I love it,' Gene said, when the last big note had been sounded. My hands were cold and clammy, a side effect of the Ritalin, and my heart was pounding. Then he said the words I had prayed for: 'Bernie, if you want to open it in the West End, I'll be glad to direct.' *Larry will be so proud of me.*

Driving home, we were hysterical with joy. We saw the standing ovation on opening night, the rave reviews, the headlines that read: '*Kasha and Hirschhorn, Heirs Apparent to the Rodgers and Hammerstein Throne.'* I didn't know then that *Copperfield* would be the single most crippling force in our lives, emotionally and creatively, for the next ten years. I certainly didn't know it when I raced across the lawn and woke Ceil up to share the incredible details of our evening at Gene's house. Joel and Jill were awake half the night dwelling on the future glory and recognition about to come our way.

I was a dedicated writer and an executive who dreaded his job. Tension headaches became routine and I would often cry out from the pain. During this time I had dinner with Janis Joplin, her manager Albert Grossman, and the president of Kama Sutra Records, Artie Ripp. The selection of a run-down Chinese restaurant on Hollywood Boulevard was odd, but it was Janis' favourite. She pulled up in a limousine, and I was surprised to see how small she was. The huge feather hat and the heavy shawl seemed to overwhelm her. Throughout dinner she drank neat vodka and talked vaguely about getting into movies. 'Can you get me a part?' she asked, her eyes protected by dark sunglasses.

I said I would try. I was a tremendous fan of her talent, and felt she would be electrifying on film if a director could be found who would tone her down for the camera.

Though she appeared shaky and distracted, I was totally unprepared to hear of her heroin overdose only a day later.

Her death hit me hard. I had barely known her, but I identified with the pressures that had driven her to destruction. I kept picturing her sad face under the huge hat and her unexpectedly small, vulnerable body.

One night in desperation, riddled with pills, dead tired and dizzy, I took a long walk past Moorpark Street, up to Laurel Canyon. I felt hypnotically drawn towards Mulholland Drive, an area that overlooked the entire city. When I arrived there, the splash of coloured Los Angeles lights glittered below. Above, the night sky was overcrowded with stars. I felt I was watching a light show especially designed by God.

I hadn't realised the depths of my despair until I stood over the edge of the canyon. How easy, I thought, to jump; to vanish into the blazingly impersonal lights; to disappear.

'Hey, mate, are you all right?'

I couldn't make out the driver's face, but his voice sounded reassuring.

'I'm fine, thanks.'

'Are you sure?'

'I'm sure.'

He drove off.

I stepped back. God was looking out for me, after all, even if I had momentarily lost grip of myself.

I prayed for guidance, then spoke into the solitary darkness: 'If I return to being solely a freelance writer, my income will be erratic, changeable. I can't guarantee Ceil and Dana the regular financial security they deserve.'

I rubbed my eyes. The flickering lights were too bright. My fingers delved through empty pockets; nervous agents searching for a pill to calm me.

Ceil was watching *The Tonight Show* when I returned at 12.30. 'Where were you?' she asked anxiously. I seldom took long nocturnal strolls.

'Mulholland Drive. Honey, I wonder—how would you feel if I never took on another executive position?'

'I wouldn't care.'

'The going could get rough. But if Joel and I just concentrated on writing, on *Copperfield*; if we gave it all we had, I *know*. . .'

'I know too,' Ceil said, putting a finger to my lips. 'You're a writer. That's all you want to do, isn't it?'

'Yes. But the life of a writer. . .'

'Is what?' She laughed, as if talking to a child. 'Hey, this is Ceil you're talking to, remember? I worked for a publisher. I know all about writers and what they go through.

And what's a little struggle anyway? Nothing at all for Ceil Batista from Gunhill Road and the Bronx.'

We heard a squeal from Dana's bedroom.

'Is she crying?' I asked.

'That's not crying,' said Ceil, embracing me before running off to attend to our daughter. 'That's a cheer. She's telling her daddy to go for it!'

# 11

# *Addicted*

I was half-convinced, but the blaring static of my thoughts kept me awake most of the night. Then at 6.30 am I heard Ceil's gasp.

The room was shaking.

For a few seconds I couldn't comprehend what was happening until I heard Ceil wail, 'Oh, God, the baby!' She raced to Dana's room as the house trembled in the grip of a powerful epileptic seizure. Dishes fell from shelves, smashing to bits; doors flew as though I had been catapulted back to Brooklyn, to my room above the subway. For an instant I was lying next to Larry, listening to my parents try to kill each other.

My bed rolled and bashed against a wall. Plaster rained on the rug. I remembered what I had read: stand between the door frames. I beckoned to Ceil, who was carrying our sobbing daughter in her arms, and we huddled together by the front door, waiting for the earth to stop dancing.

It was 9th February 1971.

The shaking stopped, only to be followed minutes later by an aftershock as powerful as the initial tremor. More dishes broke. Down the road I heard a woman's cry.

When the quake was over and we heard about the deaths in Sylmar, about the collapsing bridges and shattered roads, the billion dollars' worth of damage, Ceil and I stared at each other. It could have all been over. One of us, all of us, could have died. Just like that.

There were no guarantees, yet I had fallen into the trap of playing it safe, hanging onto a dream of security.

'I'll never stick with something I don't want, ever again,' I swore to myself. I was a writer and it was wrong, a death to the spirit, for me to be anything else.

I gathered enough courage to shake off a lifetime fear of driving and took the test. I passed it, but the uneasiness remained. I tended to clutch the steering wheel so hard that my knuckles ached. I couldn't shake my premonition of disaster.

Disaster came, on 1st July 1971.

The setting was an empty side street quite close to my home, deceptively calm and safe. I remember I was mentally reworking one of the *Copperfield* lyrics when I drew up to a stop sign. After pausing I crossed the junction and a Ford station wagon ploughed into my Toyota.

The police were on the scene in minutes. The woman who hit me, a middle-aged, overweight blonde, kept muttering, 'Have you finished now? My ice cream is melting.' I thought at first that she was in shock, but it turned out the melting ice cream *was* her prime concern.

I kept hearing her shrill voice, repeating: 'My ice cream is melting, my ice cream is melting,' and the absurdity of it made me laugh—an excruciating process, since laughter aggravated the shooting pains in my chest.

The final results for me were whiplash, hairline fracture and dislocated back. My car was written off and I realised later what a miracle it was that I hadn't been killed.

God, graciously, had intervened again.

But all I could think of, beyond the heavy sedation administered by my prescription-happy doctor, was: *I'm losing work time. Copperfield has to be rewritten. There are artists out there who need songs. I can't afford to be idle.*

I remembered a quote I had once read by Brian Epstein: 'My idea of heaven is to have ten hits in a row in the charts.' *I know what you mean*, I thought, forgetting subsequent revelations about Epstein's life: the tortured ambition, the drinking and pill-taking, the insatiable need for more and more acclaim.

Pills were also becoming my refuge. Sleeping pills—Valium, Tuinal, Percodan and Darvon—to obliterate the pain that plagued me from the accident; pain resulting from not allowing myself a proper recuperative period. Fanaticism about weight made me gobble diet pills to suppress my appetite. I couldn't manage a single day without one crutch or another, and my dependence deepened.

'Just rest a *few* days,' Ceil begged, but I ignored her advice. Joel and I met daily and stepped up our work pace. I was thirty-four, one year from thirty-five, six years from forty. Time hovered more threateningly than ever. How could I catch up with Rodgers and Hammerstein, Neil Diamond (whose first records I had produced), Goffin and King, if I lost an hour here, an hour there?

We received a letter from Delfont, agreeing to produce *Copperfield* with Gene Kelly directing. He began to scout around for available West End theatres when Gene suddenly became unavailable. 'There's a personal problem,' was the most specific line we could elicit from his secretary, Lois.

Not long after, Gene's wife, Jeannie, was dead from leukemia. It was a heartbreaking blow.

We had observed, at close range, the genuine feeling and affection between them; the sort of unostentatious love and warmth that filled onlookers with vicarious pleasure. The tenderness they shared had been one reason why visiting the red house on Rodeo Drive had been so pleasant and memorable. They had two young children: a boy, Timothy, and a girl, Bridget. Gene would have to bring them up alone.

London, of course, was out of the question now.

Around this time, Larry directed a Broadway musical, *Lovely Ladies and Kind Gentlemen*, based on *Teahouse of the*

*August Moon*. It closed after a short run. I felt sorry for Larry and rationalised that the theatre was a murderous racket, and who wanted to go to New York anyway? I was lying to myself. The theatre bug, sparked at seven years old, still burned in me.

In the meantime, while searching for a new producer and director, Joel and I used *Copperfield* as our audition piece. One of the impressed listeners was a man named Happy Goday. Wiry, dynamic, always in motion, Happy ranked among the industry's top five publishers. I had known him since my CBS days and had cut many songs for him, notably 'As Long as He Needs Me', 'Cotton Fields' and 'Who Can I Turn To?'. Now based primarily in Hollywood, Happy heard that Twentieth Century Fox wanted a theme song for their blockbuster production of the year, *The Poseidon Adventure*. Every writer in town, apparently, had submitted something and had been turned down. The producers were in a panic.

A long shot, but we met with the record company president Russ Regan, studio music head Lionel Newman, director Ronald Neame, and producer Irwin Allen. They handed us a script and told us to 'go home and bring something in by nine in the morning'.

Not having seen the film presented a handicap, so we tested a thousand different alternatives, recalling director Ronald Neame's request that 'the lyric content must be positive'. This task was not easy when an ocean liner is about to be demolished and most of the cast members drowned in photogenically ghoulish ways.

'Make it a love song,' said producer Irwin Allen, presenting a further challenge in the face of so much disaster.

At 4.00am, Joel started writing shorthand ideas in the air. My patience was gone by then and I yelled, 'If you have a line, write it on *paper*.'

Joel nodded, erased the mid-air thought with a swift jerk of his palm, and made a note of it on a pad.

By 5.30 our nerves were frayed, and we were snapping at each other—one of the few displays of outward temper in our career.

'I *still* think the last verse could be stronger,' I insisted.

'It's fine,' said Joel.

'One note change, just *one* note.'

'I think the note makes it hard to remember. It's illogical.'

'It's too obvious the other way.'

Our differences of opinion subsided by 7.30, and 'The Morning After' emerged. Joel never made it home. We had a quick breakfast with Jill and Ceil before driving, in a sleepless haze, to the Twentieth Century Fox building.

All the way to Century City we sang the song, analysing it to make sure it was the best we could do. We were anxious but satisfied. The writing of the lyric had been tremendously helped by some advice I'd once received from Johnny Mercer in New York: 'Don't tell the story— tell the feelings *behind* the action.' Every line we wrote related to the plot, without spelling it out:

> There's got to be a morning after,
> If we can hold on through the night.
> We have a chance to find the sunshine;
> Let's keep on looking for the light.

Our imagery—bridges, lights, darkness—had some connection to plot events, but we made no reference to the actual shipwreck, or to a cast of characters forced to climb through an upside-down ocean liner.

I also felt, without knowing quite why, that the song should have a sense of hope, a spiritual undercurrent. My past had been so negative that I automatically projected Hammerstein 'cock-eyed optimist' flavour into lyrics.

We staggered into Lionel Newman's office at 8.30 the next morning. Joel had barely learned the melody and hit a few wrong notes. I was asleep on my feet, and my voice croaked on the high notes. At the conclusion there was a deafening silence.

'Want us to play it again?' I asked.

They nodded. This time I sang with more authority, and Joel supplied a background voice to add power.

'Hmmm,' Ronald Neame said, turning to Irwin Allen. 'I believe it has something. What do you think?'

After a long pause, Irwin Allen smiled and said, 'Let's go with it.'

As filming commenced, I thought about how far we'd come from the Pink Cloud.

'Maybe we'll even be nominated for an Oscar,' I said to Joel. He smiled that familiar I'll-let-him-fantasise smile, but I could tell he was hoping too.

The spiritual quality of 'The Morning After' was picked up by a lighting man on the *Poseidon* set, a man named Mark, who walked up to me and said, 'You know you've written a Christian song. That lyric could have been written for God.'

And he quoted:

> It's not too late—we should be giving.
> Only with love can we climb.
> It's not too late—not while we're living.
> Let's put our hands out in time.

I thought of the lighting man, Mark, and the peace he radiated. He was young, with wheat-coloured hair and green eyes. What struck me most was the relaxed air he projected; he seemed totally in tune with himself. I envied that peace.

I ran into Mark again at the Twentieth Century Fox office, and he invited me to join him for lunch. When our sandwiches arrived, I reached for mine, but the look in Mark's eyes made me hesitate.

'Do you mind if we pray first?' he asked. I said 'no' and Mark whispered thanks for the food, for the day and for all the blessings in his life.

'You know, Mark,' I said, after a few minutes, 'you always seem so together. What's your secret?'

'My faith,' he said simply. The gentle conviction of his tone rose above office clamour. 'You know, I have Bible classes in my home every Tuesday. Why don't you come to one?'

'I'm Jewish.'

'I know.'

'It's not that I don't think Jesus was a great man. . . a great rabbi. . . a great force for good,' I found myself stuttering, trying to explain.

'He's more than that.'

Mark put his hand on my sleeve. His grip was strong, full of pressure. 'I can only tell you that Jesus changed my life. You wouldn't believe what I was like five years ago. . . strung out on drugs all the time, missing work, never sleeping . . . and always bitter. And this town doesn't help. Hollywood can bury you if you don't have an anchor. . . if you don't have Jesus. Without him, this town will eat you alive.' He hesitated. 'You think I'm crazy.'

'No I don't.'

'It's just that you wrote that spiritual song and I felt. . . a searching. A need.'

Mark's serene and tranquil image remained with me in the days ahead. I mentioned him to a drummer I knew. 'I bet he doesn't have a trouble in the world,' I said.

'Are you kidding? Mark lost his three-year-old son last year. The baby was born with a defective heart, and they gave him all kinds of operations, but he died anyway. I don't know what my wife and I would have done if it had been us.'

I recalled Mark saying, 'My Father is with me all the time.' Could his faith really have eased the pain of such a tragedy?

I decided to go to one of Mark's Bible classes. But Joel and I became busy with *Copperfield* and I couldn't find the time.

'...there were once two brothers from Brooklyn ... Tony Award winner
Larry Kasha and Academy Award winner Al Kasha.'

*Al Kasha, Gene Kelly and Joel Hirschhorn at the
Academy Awards (second Oscar).*

*Joel Hirschhorn, Mickey Rooney and Al Kasha.*

*Larry Kasha with Barbra Streisand at the opening of the musical 'Funny Girl' in London.*

*Al Kasha, guest speaker at the Hollywood Walk-of-Fame ceremony, honouring his close friend, singer Donna Summer in March 1992.*

*Al Kasha, Cher, Sonny Bono and Joel Hirschhorn at the Academy Awards in 1972.*

# 12

## *Oscar*

After *The Poseidon Adventure*, Ceil and I felt secure enough to buy a home in Beverly Hills. For all its rustic charm, however (aptly conveyed by our address 'Shirley Lane'), I felt the house was rather small. But Ceil said, 'Just leave it to me. When I've finished with it we'll have a show house.'

Ceil had a decorator's eye (she had already expressed an interest in pursuing home design professionally) and I decided to trust her instincts. She ripped up carpeting, steamed down wallpaper, and slowly turned Shirley Lane into a hilltop paradise. In 1975, Los Angeles' *Home Magazine* did a piece on her work, with a picture of 'the 40-foot garden which she floored with Italian tile and bedecked with white wicker furniture and scores of plants'.

Her sense of decor and colour was soothing—and I needed the soothing solitude it provided, because my emotional world was growing more chaotic. Every phone call from my parents tied me tighter to the bonds of achievement. My mother only had to say, 'How are you, L'Alfred?' and I felt compelled to issue a full report, embellishing the truth until she was satisfied.

'I'm doing a new film, Mum.'

'I have three records in the charts, Mum.'

'Joel and I are doing a show, Mum.'

'How's that, Mum?'

I sensed a dangerous desperation growing and it related directly to *Copperfield*. The project had begun to represent my overall worth; a yardstick to measure success or failure. Common sense warned me about the perils of investing so much energy in one show, but I couldn't help it. Prestige, fame, wealth, Larry's respect, enthusiasm from my parents—all, I felt, would be mine if this one production got off the ground. I would be my brother's equal. The left eye would attain the stature of the right eye.

Sir Delfont fed the anxiety by wiring us: 'Still interested in *Copperfield* for West End next year, if proper director can be found to replace Gene Kelly.' I compiled a list of possibilities and sent it to London.

A month dragged by with no response. We were told that Delfont had gone on holiday, then a business trip to France, then to visit a sick member of his family.

Other symptoms of emotional breakdown appeared and intensified. I found I couldn't enjoy a film unless it related to my work. There had to be a 'reason' to see it. Could I learn from it? I sat in darkened cinemas as a pupil, tearing apart the lighting, editing, scoring and performances.

There's nothing wrong with this kind of self-education; creative people are perpetually hungry for knowledge. But when you cross a line, as I did, and find yourself unable to respond purely as a spectator, the whole process becomes a chore—like cramming for exams at school on subjects you hate.

The *Copperfield* saga continued. Our friend, Irwin Kostal, arranger of *West Side Story*, *The Sound of Music* and *Mary Poppins*, offered inspiration and encouragement.

With Irwin in our corner, I redoubled my efforts on behalf of *Copperfield*. Happy introduced us to producer Arthur Jacobs. Slim, hyperactive and dapper, Arthur was a former press agent for Gary Cooper and Marilyn Monroe; a man who adored show business. He also adored musicals, and had done three by the time we met him: *Dr Dolittle*, *Tom Sawyer* and *Goodbye, Mr Chips*.

'Play him *Copperfield*,' Happy suggested.

We did, and his first response was, 'Can I produce it?' I pointed out that Sir Delfont owned the rights. Arthur wasted no time. What was Delfont's number? When could we finish the script? Where did we feel it should be shot? 'Ireland,' he went on, without waiting for a reply. 'In the summer. And I know the perfect guy to do the set—Tony Walton.'

He meant it. A day later he reached Delfont, and a week later he had purchased the rights from Delfont for $35,000, which was $30,000 more than Delfont had paid for them in the first place.

'Just think, Ireland,' I told Joel. 'A musical of our own— book, words and music. Think of what this will do for us in the industry.'

A minor stumbling-block slowed us down. Joel's wife, Jill, had written an original show, *Rainbow Jones*, and needed an accompanist for the first two weeks of local performances. Jill didn't want to hire anyone—felt Joel had the right pianistic touch—and he agreed to help out.

The show's cast members included Richard Dreyfuss, Lee Merriwether and Betty Garrett and it had strong potential. The only trouble was, rehearsals ate into our writing time.

'Arthur needs these rewrites in a week,' I told Joel. 'We'll lose this chance. *I'll* pay for an accompanist.'

'It's the least I can do, as her husband,' Joel said. 'We'll be able to get the work done.'

I might have overreacted to the situation from my own vantage point. I had a problem with the idea of wives with careers, whether they held secretarial jobs or wrote Broadway musicals. My mother had been a working wife, had devoted her main energy to the shop, and I blamed that for her inadequacies as a homemaker.

I wanted my wife to be at home when I got there.

'Al,' Ceil said one evening, 'I'd like to go back to work.'

She said it casually, but I felt myself stiffen.

'In fact, I'd like to open a shop with my friend Barbara.'

Mistaking my silence for agreement, Ceil rushed on: 'And we thought we'd call it Setting Up House. What do you think of the name?'

*I don't like the name. I don't like the whole idea. I'm not on Avenue M any more!*

'Honey, why do you have to work?'

'Well, I had a job before we got married. And you're busy with Joel. I can't just sit around with a four-year-old all day. And I'll be at home in the morning and evening.' She was talking too fast, running her words together. 'If I don't like it—if it interferes with us—I'll give up the whole thing. I just want to try.'

'My mother worked in a shop.'

'I'm not your mother.'

'It's Rose and Irving's all over again.'

'That's not fair.'

'All over again.'

'Your mother was a selfish woman. I'm not like her.'

'You'll *become* like her!'

I saw that Ceil was hurt.

'I love you,' she said quietly. 'I'd never do anything to jeopardise our marriage.'

'A shop can take over your whole life.'

'It won't.'

'OK,' I said, though every bone in my body ached with opposition. 'Try it for a couple of months. But if it gets in the way, you'll give up, won't you?'

'Yes.'

I kept pace with my Brill Building friends. Carole King was a recording star and Neil Sedaka was in the midst of a comeback on Elton John's Rocket records. But Gerry Goffin (now divorced from Carole) was relatively inactive. Mann and Weil were burned out from the non-stop, night-

and-day work regimen, and Jack Keller was struggling. We had maintained a relentless pace since our teens and now, in our mid-thirties, we were physically and emotionally exhausted. I wondered what kept us all going, and which of us would crack first.

'The Morning After' was nominated for an Oscar. No one thought it stood a chance against 'Ben', a Number One hit for Michael Jackson, written by veterans Walter Scharf and Don Black.

My old friend Jackie Wilson called after reading the news. Jackie had been through many professional ups and downs. His hits stopped in the late 1960s, after the artistic and commercial high of his smash 'Your Love Keeps Lifting Me (Higher and Higher)', but he sounded as positive and powerful as ever.

'Man, I *know* you're gonna take it,' he said, and his conviction made it easier to dismiss the majority viewpoint.

My mother's good wishes were, as always, couched in anxiety. 'Oh, darling, I'll die if you don't win,' she moaned. 'I'm going to the temple tonight to pray, and I'll go there every day until the Oscar show.'

Arthur Jacobs unwittingly added further pressure on us when he said, 'If you win, it'll give *Copperfield* a much better chance for success.' Coincidentally, Larry was opening his new musical, *Seesaw*, on Broadway at the same time. My mother spoke proudly of 'both my sons'. 'Both my sons are going to be famous,' she repeated, over and over again, and I thought of all the times Larry and I had shared things: a room, a bed, credit.

I won.

And Larry's show opened to good reviews.

*It's a tie!*

*Why am I fighting?* I asked myself when I got home. *I know it's an incredible victory. I know it will help me with my peers. I know Irwin Allen and Lionel Newman are delighted.*

I wanted to cry.

I felt old, prematurely old. I would have given anything to be a child. I felt as though I were scaling a hill that kept growing steeper with every step I took. I thought of Gypsy Rose Lee's mother singing 'Rose's Turn', and her plaintive question: 'What Did I Do It For?'

I didn't know the answer, yet the image of *David Copperfield* hung over me—a patchwork of Dickensian characters, taunting me in shrill, ridiculing tones: the irresponsible Micawber, stern Aunt Betsey, harsh Mr Murdstone hitting David.

*He had my head in a vice, but I twined round him somehow, and stopped him for a moment, entreating him not to beat me. . . .*

He beat me then, as if he would have beaten me to death. . . .

I was lying, feverish and hot, and torn, and sore, and raging in my puny way, upon the floor.

Dickens knew. He understood.


'The Morning After' became Number One around the world with Maureen McGovern. Maureen had been a secretary from Cleveland, Ohio, with no recordings to her credit. This debut record made her an instant star.

Timing helped too. The nation was still euphoric, coasting on a wave of hope following Presidents' Nixon's announcement on 27th January that the war in Vietnam was over. "The Morning After" spoke optimistically of the future, underlining the national mood. Watergate had begun, but no one fully realised its seriousness yet.

'Your Oscar is nothing,' Arthur Jacobs assured Joel and me. '*Copperfield* will make "The Morning After" look like chopped liver.'

He outlined plans to take on Herb Ross as director. His production man, he said, had even found the site of the 1851 London Exhibition; most of the exhibits from that event had been preserved. 'We can shoot the whole thing for $3 million,' he announced exultantly.

Ceil and I were making preparations for a stay in Ireland. Gene Kelly's descriptions of the beautiful countryside had whetted my appetite, and I was reading a *Hollywood Reporter* announcement about *Copperfield* when my phone rang. It was Lionel Newman.

'Hey, I'm sorry to tell you this mate, but Arthur's dead.'

The *Reporter* fell from my hand.

'Middle of the night. . . massive coronary. . . a shame, only fifty-two years old.' Lionel kept talking, though I only heard bits and pieces.

Arthur had been a popular man, and hundreds of friends clustered together for his funeral at the Hillside Chapel in Culver City. With morbid, uncharacteristic ESP, Joel had dreamed the night before that Arthur had been killed in a car crash. He had been wrong about the particulars, but the dream's accuracy was chilling.

Joel and I began to feel threatened—there's no other word for it—when we read in *Variety* a few days later that Sean Kenny, the designer Gene had chosen to do *Copperfield*, had died in his sleep.

'Is this project jinxed?' Joel wondered aloud.

*We can beat the odds*, I thought. As always when confronted with a challenge, my determination grew.

# 13

## *The Towering Inferno*

*Copperfield* continued on its brutally bumpy course. United Artists president David Picker took an option on it, then left the company. Director Peter Medak (who had done a critically acclaimed film, *The Ruling Class*) was eager to tackle it, until United Artists ruled him out.

Lightning struck twice when *Poseidon* producer Irwin Allen called one Monday and asked Joel and me to write a love song for another disaster film, *The Towering Inferno*. Only catch: he wanted it on Tuesday.

We went to work, reading the script, living through the same pressure we had experienced on 'The Morning After'. 'Black coffee coming up,' said Ceil, as we struggled to finish 'We May Never Love Like This Again'.

Allen liked the song. It came down to a competition between our song and one Fred Astaire (one of the film's cast members) had written. To our great relief, we were the final choice.

'We May Never Love Like This Again' was nominated for an Oscar. The ceremonies were as nerve-wracking as before, but there was great personal pleasure in being presented our *Towering Inferno* awards by Shirley MacLaine and Gene Kelly. Gene had specifically requested our category, feeling we had the best chance to win. Another friend from my Columbia days, Aretha Franklin, sang the song.

Aretha and I spoke at the Academy Awards banquet afterwards, and she seemed to be glowing and full of optimism. Before we parted, she was gracious enough to say, 'Best of luck, honey. You deserve that award.'

My mother's words were less palatable, more anxiety-provoking. 'I prayed for you to win,' she said. 'I stayed all night in the temple. How I prayed, "Let my Alfred make it. I know someday he'll make it. Someday he'll be famous." '

*What do you mean, someday? What do you mean, you're praying I'll make it? I won a second Oscar last night!*

Domestic clouds began to build up. I had never got over wishing Ceil would abandon her business and stay at home, and when Setting Up House proved a disappointment, I expected her to give her full concentration to our joint goals. Instead she told me, 'I had lunch with Jackie Mazur. We talked about going into partnership.'

Jackie was a good friend, wife of Billy Joel's manager Irwin Mazur, a busy interior decorater on her own.

'Why work?' I asked her. 'Don't I make enough money? You don't *need* to work.'

'I told you, I have to keep busy. But it won't be a shop. I'll make my own hours. I'll work out of the house. You won't even know I'm working.'

*I'll know*, I thought. But I acquiesced.

Joel was experiencing tension too. Jill's musical, *Rainbow Jones* (for which she had written book, words and music), was set to open on Broadway at the Music Box Theatre. It had received superb reviews in Boston and Washington, but I felt its fanciful Charlie Brown charm would be out of place in a large Broadway theatre. Even though Peter Kastner was brash and appealing in the Richard Dreyfuss part, the critics decided it wasn't Broadway-type material. The difficulty was best expressed by a woman in the audience, who whispered to her companion, 'Where are the dancing girls?'

Jill's work as lyricist, librettist and tune writer was outstanding. Since merit wasn't the issue, I had to look elsewhere, and *Rainbow Jones* taught me that every genre has its rules: rock 'n' roll was aggressive; films were a visual rather than dialogue medium; Broadway musicals emphasised opulence and production values over subtlety. We had to make sure that when *Copperfield* arrived in New York, it had the right 'look'; eye-filling costumes, imaginative lighting, expansive choreography.

I tried to hide my growing despair by socialising. Ceil arranged a joint birthday party for Ernest Borgnine and me at Ernie's house. He and I had been friends since *The Poseidon Adventure*, and I enjoyed his genial charm and urbane wit, qualities far removed from either the vicious Fatso of *From Here to Eternity* or the inarticulate butcher of *Marty*.

Ceil and I also liked his wife, Tove. The two of them reminded me of Irving Mansfield and Jacqueline Susann. Tove had gone into the cosmetics business, with Ernie's full approval and backing, and had succeeded at it. They were mutually supportive of each other. At the party Ernie confided, 'I found the right woman. She's for me, I'm for her. When you've got that, you've got everything.'

During this period Joel and I acquired an image. Immediately following *The Towering Inferno*, Frank Capra, Jr asked us, on the recommendation of scorer David Shire, to supply the music for a two-hour TV film *Trapped Beneath the Sea*. The papers later announced: 'Masters of Disaster Al Kasha and Joel Hirschhorn to Score Telemovie.' Columnist Dianne Bennett picked up the phrase and referred to the 'Masters of Disaster' in her column, and from then on we were branded with that name.

The phrase also seemed an apt description of my private life when I learned that my parents were planning to fly to California to stay with us for a month.

I was in my mid-thirties, but my father's animal brutality still made me uneasy. After crushing my hand, he pounded my back. 'Stop that,' I said, too sharply, and he grinned. My quick response let him know he was still a threatening presence. His grin also announced, *I'm stronger than you are. I can beat you anytime.*

His strength amazed me. Nothing slowed him down—not the diabetes he had developed or the morning vodka he combined with herring.

'He's worse than ever,' my mother confided, clutching my arm possessively to underscore the point. She indicated a scar on her forehead; a scar that stood out clearly above the plastered-on make-up. 'Mr Weinberger next door had to come and stop him from killing me,' she said. 'He would have killed me, Alfred. What can I do?'

I had heard this so many times. Her pleas for help, for rescue, before forgiving him and lapsing into the old pattern. I thought of all our conversations by the till in the shop—the promises I had made to give her a better life.

'Ma,' I said—it seemed so clear, suddenly—'why not move here?'

'Your father doesn't like it. He wants to stay in Brooklyn.'

'Not with Daddy. Just you.'

'I can't do that.'

'Why can't you? Don't worry about the money. I have money. I can find you a nice flat, and you'll be free of him. He won't hurt you any more.'

'So quick. . . just leave?'

'What do you mean, so quick? Yes, leave. Leave it all behind. You hate him. He's made your life a misery for forty-six years. Do it.'

'I'll have to see.'

'You keep saying that. What's to stop you?'

'L'Alfred. . .'

'Alfred!'

'Alfred, he's still my husband.'

'He beats you. He drinks. He's crazy. He's made life miserable for all of us—you and me and Larry. You've always talked about the way out. This is it.'

'Someday, when the time is right.'

'Ma, you're sixty-eight years old.'

I couldn't understand her reluctance. She had been delaying this decision since my childhood, waiting for the 'right time'. . . when she could afford it. . . when we were successful. . . when they retired.

'Alfred, save me.'

'Ma, I'm trying to save you, but you won't let me. If you don't leave him now, you never will. And you'll hate yourself for not taking the chance. For never having lived.'

She promised she would think about it, and nothing more was said.

Ceil and I did our best to entertain my parents. By this time Ceil's decorating career with Jackie had taken off, a partnership that would eventually bring in such clients as Ernie Borgnine, Nell Carter, Donna Summer, Dom De Luise and Stephanie Powers. She put aside her growing business obligations and took them to the cinema, to Disneyland and Universal, and to department stores for new clothes.

Our friends, producer Jack Wohl and his wife Micki, invited us to dinner and we took my parents along. Micki thoughtfully prepared a Jewish meal, and in the familiar atmosphere of matzo, potato pancakes and chicken, my father denounced 'these lousy *goyim*. . . do you know they used to beat me up when I was a boy in Poland?'. Ceil held her tongue. Later on my mother called Micki 'the perfect daughter-in-law to have—a wonderful cook, a nice Jewish girl'—and the other rage sprang up again.

They refused to give Ceil her due—or Dana either, beyond my mother's observation, 'She's gorgeous, L'Alfred. . . she looks like me.' My brother called and announced he was moving to Los Angeles. 'I've got to get away from the theatre for a while,' he told me. 'I want to produce films.'

Flying from Avenue M was pointless; Avenue M was flying to meet me.

Larry came to Los Angeles on a Friday. One day later he asked me to have lunch with him at the Brown Derby on Hollywood and Vine.

Since I had never been first on my brother's list, I wondered why this lunch was so important.

I arrived at the restaurant first. When Larry walked in, there was something peculiarly purposeful about his stride. His greeting was warmer, more open than normal.

'Welcome to California,' I said, trying to sound enthusiastic.

He ordered carrot juice and I ordered a Diet Coke.

'I saw a house yesterday, believe it or not,' Larry said. 'My friend Clay—he's an editor at Paramount—showed me this divine place on Gloaming Way. It overlooks Mulholland Drive and the view is magnificent.'

He rattled on about the possibilities of the house, but I got the feeling it was only a prelude.

A tall, slim waiter in his early twenties walked by and stared at Larry. Larry, as though feeling the intensity of his stare, turned around and smiled.

'I have to join a gym,' Larry said. 'Can't let the pounds pile up.'

There was little worry of that. Larry had maintained his perfect physique since the Catskill Mountains. If anything, he was thinner now.

'We're going to be living in the same city,' Larry said, 'and it's not like New York. . . it's more suburban. In Hollywood things. . . get around.'

'Are you ready to order?' said the waiter, crashing in on a crucial moment.

'In just a few minutes,' said Larry.

I drank my entire jumbo glass of Diet Coke in one gulp, feeling nervous. I didn't want to hear what was coming—but nothing could stop it.

'I'm sure you know about my. . . lifestyle. You know I'm gay.'

I nodded.

'I've been walking a tightrope for years,' Larry said. 'Playing it straight. . . being the confirmed bachelor who might one day get married.'

For a moment he seemed self-conscious, but he plunged ahead.

'I'm in love. His name is Darryl. Darryl London. He's a scriptwriter, and we're doing a screenplay together. He hasn't had anything produced yet, but his talent is incredible.' Then, after catching his breath: 'This is the relationship I've been waiting for all my life.'

'Are you sure?'

'Absolutely.'

'What about when you wanted to marry Peggy?'

'I was just acting. . . trying to be something I wasn't.'

'Wouldn't you have got married if Mother hadn't talked you out of it?'

Larry wanted my unqualified understanding and approval; he didn't want me to analyse or question. But I couldn't just say, 'Fine, be happy and be gay.'

'Have you. . . ever talked to anyone about this?'

I knew it was a mistake to say that, even before the question was uttered.

'Al, I'm not sick and I don't want to be cured.'

The subject was dropped. For the rest of the meal we ate in silence. I could see that Larry fiercely regretted opening himself up to me.

'I'd like to meet Darryl,' I said, trying to undo the damage.

'Maybe someday,' he answered, grabbing the bill and paying it. 'My schedule is absolutely impossible for the next month.'

The temperature was 102 degrees, with smog so chokingly thick I couldn't breathe. My mother complained: 'You call this wonderful? It's worse than New York.'

We were lounging by the pool; Dana toyed with a mop handle. I stared at the handle, vaguely preoccupied with it, not making any specific connections. My father sat back in his deckchair, shirt off to reveal a still muscular chest.

'Grandpa,' Dana said. 'Play with me.'

'Go to your grandmother,' he answered, still facing the sun.

'Grandpa, I want to play with *you*.'

'Come over here, Dana,' Ceil ordered. Dana didn't move. There was a moment of dead silence—the kind of unnatural silence that precedes an explosion—then Dana, swinging the mop handle, accidentally hit my father in the leg with it.

He leaped up wordlessly, a puppet programmed to do one thing. . . strike out. I watched in horror as that hated hand smashed my daughter's face. She fell to the ground screaming.

In a split second I was on my feet, grabbing him, punching him with insane force. I couldn't believe that old, brutal Avenue M scenes had spilled into the second generation.

*OK, big shot. How do you like that, big shot?*

Dana was inconsolable. Ceil fought to placate her.

'You're never, *never* to lay a hand on my daughter again, or I'll kill you,' I shouted. 'Never touch her again.'

'She was. . . hitting me,' he protested.

'She's five years old. *Five years old*.'

'I didn't hit her hard,' he said, as though he and Dana were physical equals and contemporaries.

'Five years old,' I repeated. My voice was weird, inhuman; an unearthly sound echoing through the neat, manicured Beverly Hills garden.

'Five years old.'

'Al, it's all right,' Ceil said, frightened now. I was out of control. I could only utter those words again and again, while my father insisted, 'I had to teach her a lesson,' my mother sobbed, and Ceil held on to me in the dimming afternoon light.

My parents left in the morning, but I didn't calm down. Phobic symptoms returned and multiplied. My pill dependence was reaching crisis proportions. Nightmares of being thrown into a wardrobe returned. I woke up, chilled and soaked simultaneously, after terrifying visions of being beaten and covered in blood. Sometimes I screamed myself awake, and Ceil had to hold me for an hour before I regained control. Later she would describe to me the gasping, moaning sounds I made while in the grip of panic.

Often I'd tiptoe into Dana's room and watch her sleep, studying her peaceful expression, reassuring myself desperately that she was safe. *Please don't let her be scarred by that experience*, I pleaded. *Don't let the sight of my father's violent hand burn a permanent scar on her memory.*

Sometimes I sang 'The Morning After' to her quietly in the darkness:

> Oh, can't you see the morning after?
> It's waiting right outside the storm.
> Why don't we cross the bridge together
> And find a place that's safe and warm?

I would seize the rim of the bed and swear, 'My father's father beat him up, my father beat me up, and now he has hit my daughter. I swear, the chain stops here. No one will lay a hand on my daughter again.'

Once Dana woke up and saw me standing over her.

'What's wrong, Daddy?'

'I'm just checking up on you, darling. Are you all right?'

Her sleepy eyes met mine and said, 'I'm fine.'

I kissed her and went back to bed, praying she really was.

I had always dreaded driving, avoiding it whenever possible. Now I found I would begin to choke on the road; I would hyperventilate and have to pull over. I had never been entirely comfortable in restaurants; now I refused to enter one unless a business meeting demanded it.

These attacks of fear infuriated me. I thought of myself as strong, a leader, and I was dominated by terrors that pounced on me unexpectedly and made each day a new nightmare. The palpitations, which had ceased for a few months, assaulted me now with the intensity of a heart attack.

'Let's go and see a film,' Ceil would suggest. 'It'll do you good.' I pleaded exhaustion.

'I can't get over what my father did,' I said.

There was a long pause.

'It didn't only happen to you, Al,' she said. 'It happened to me too. And most of all, it happened to Dana.'

I felt defensive. They were my parents; it was my history. I was the only one they had destroyed with their cruelty.

She began to sob bitterly.

'It'll be all right,' I said, putting out my arms.

She avoided the embrace. 'It won't be all right unless you give up the past. You have to let go of your old family. Dana and I are your family now.'

'I know that.'

'You *don't* know it,' Ceil cried. 'You hang on, you keep hoping they'll change. They won't change. And as long as you make them the centre of everything, we can't live a decent life.'

She began to pace. 'Forget me. What about your daughter? Do you *see* her? Do you know how she's doing at school? Do you know her friends? Do you even know she has been sick with the flu all week?'

'She had a cold.'

'She had *flu*. And that's another thing. You're not the

only person in this house who gets ill.'

She was on the verge of hysteria now. 'I love you, but I can't stand to see what's happening to you. . . what you're *letting* happen.'

'I'm not well.'

'You're not trying to get well.'

'I love you,' I whispered. But I felt more alone than ever.

Temporary distraction arrived in the form of Bette Davis. She had contacted our agent, expressing a desire to play Aunt Betsey Trotwood when *Copperfield* became a film.

We arranged to play our score for her in the dining room of the Bel Air Hotel. Ms Davis met us in the lobby. She was surprisingly small, less imposing in person than on the screen, but we recognised her authority when I mentioned my friendship with Ernest Borgnine. 'You know,' I said, he starred in *Catered Affair* with you.' She stared imperiously, puffed her cigarette and replied, 'I remember the picture, dear. I'm not *that* old.'

'She sounds just like she did in *The Great Lie*,' Joel mumbled, then proceeded to turn into a movie fan again. He brought up a Davis double feature he'd recently seen at a nostalgia festival, *Three on a Match* and *Cabin in the Cotton*, which pleased her. Did she think, he wondered, that *Of Human Bondage* had stood the test of time? What was it like working with George Arliss? ('A *dear* man. I owe him so much.') Leslie Howard?

I kicked him under the table, to remind him that *The Great Lie* was yesterday's news and *Copperfield* was the issue.

Davis' reactions were gratifying. 'Your script is brilliant,' she said. When we modestly pointed out that Dickens had been a great help, she answered vehemently, 'But look what you *did* with him.' She applauded after every number we did.

'You can count on me for this role,' she said. I felt fresh

hope. How fantastic to have Bette Davis play a role written by us! Someone would be bound to come up with full financing if they knew she was a definite part of the package.

That night I dreamed about *Copperfield*. The characters, sometimes enemies, sometimes friends, had become so real that I carried them inside me all the time. I imagined Bette Davis as the seemingly severe but warm-hearted Aunt Betsey. If the film was ever made, she would have its strongest moment: the moment when abused, tormented young David is adopted and permanently rescued from the tyranny of his stepfather:

> ...Her face gradually relaxed and became so pleasant that I was emboldened to kiss and thank her, which I did with great heartiness, and with both my arms clasped 'round her neck.
> ...Thus I began my new life, in a new name and with everything new about me. Now that the state of doubt was over, I felt, for many days, like one in a dream.

It was a scene I never tired of reading. I felt rescued, temporarily, when I played the words over in my head.

I dreaded leaving home more and more. Agoraphobia, once held at a manageable distance, was assuming full control. Strange symptoms began to appear: a spastic colon, which caused me to double up in pain; headaches; rashes all over my body. I checked into Cedars Sinai Hospital in October 1975, and spent the week undergoing tests.

One of the doctors was a dark, burly man with thick arms. He reminded me of my father, triggering off visions of abuse. I asked for another doctor, without explaining why.

'Doctor Baker is supposed to be the best,' said Ceil.

'You've got to get me somebody else.'

While there I brooded over the fact that my mother hadn't called. It took a TV report about Jackie Wilson to divert my attention. Jackie had suffered a serious stroke during a performance at the Latin Casino in New Jersey. When I checked and discovered how serious the attack was, my depression grew worse.

'He's going to die,' I said to Ceil. 'We're all dying.' Images of the Brill Building swam in front of me. Jackie's rehearsing 'My Empty Arms' in a tacky, airless cubicle. Burt Bacharach and Hal David's singing and playing in the next room. Lieber and Stoller down the hall. *We're all middle-aged*, I thought. *Where did the time go? And what have I done in the meantime?*

'There's nothing wrong with you,' the doctors said. 'It's just nerves.' And Ceil added, 'Isn't that great? You're healthy.'

'There is something wrong,' I protested. 'They're just not finding it.'

I hated to leave the hospital; hated to leave the cocoon of sympathetic doctors and nurses.

*Copperfield* reclaimed my attention. A Canadian producer, Harold Greenberg, loved our script and score and wanted us to fly to Toronto to perform the music for some backer friends.

I went, heavily sedated. Larry joined Joel and me. He was enthusiastic. 'This is first rate,' he raved. Those words meant everything. All my life I had waited for my brother to admire my work.

'I'd like to co-produce,' he continued. 'I'll help you get the script in shape and bring in any money people Harold doesn't come up with.'

Toronto was encouraging. Harold claimed he had all the financing, and once again I told Joel, 'This time it feels right.' He agreed. I returned to the hotel, fired with excitement, and there was a message from Ceil.

'Your father is sick, Al,' she said. 'I've just heard from your mother, and she's falling apart. The doctors told her he'll be dead in six months.'

Larry and I flew to New York to see him. I thought I'd be prepared; I'd seen shrivelled, wasted cancer victims during my stay at Cedars. But it's different when the frail, emaciated near-corpse is your own father. Overnight his strength had deserted him and his handshake, so repellently powerful in the past, was feeble and limp.

'Alfred,' he said. 'My son. My son.'

He was frightened. It was odd to feel his childlike panic; odd to see him clutching me for support.

'I'm here,' I whispered. 'And I'll take care of you.' I phoned Ceil and asked her if she would mind my bringing my parents to California to live with us, until. . .

There was the briefest hesitation on the phone. Ceil was wiser than I; she knew what trouble I was courting.

'It's the least I can do for him,' I told her.

'All right. If you think it's best.'

The moment of tender self-sacrifice passed, and I realised the enormity of what I had undertaken. I remained at Avenue M for three days. All the years on my own—years that had brought me awards, acknowledgement from famous people, a shaky but growing sense of self—vanished every time I stretched out on my old bed. My Valium tablets could have been peppermints for all the power they exerted on my hotly active brain.

The underground subway still rattled and shook our building. Buses still stopped on the corner and squealed back into gear. My mother's voice droned over the noise with 'You'll Never Know'. Each note, in my tortured mind, was stretched twice or three times its proper length.

'And. . . if. . . I. . . tried. . . I. . . still. . . couldn't. . . hide. . . my. . . love. . . for. . . you. . . .'

Cockroaches had extended their previous territory beyond the kitchen and bathroom. I found one racing across my pillow.

My father's doctor cautioned me. 'He really shouldn't fly. There's arteriosclerosis as well as cancer. I *think* he can survive the trip, but I'm not sure.'

'At least he'll be in California with his sons.'

The morning of the flight, my father complained bitterly. 'I don't want to go to LA.' Helping him dress was difficult; he couldn't decide what to wear, and he maintained a running argument with my mother. Even in his broken, terminal state, his hostility for her remained strong; the strongest part of him, as it had always been.

'Let me shave you, Daddy,' I suggested, when I noticed the razor trembling in his hand.

'No!' he snapped. 'I shaved myself all my life, I can shave myself now.'

I jumped back at the jerky motion of his arm, till I remembered his condition. He couldn't hurt me. His power was gone.

'You're cutting your chin.'

'What's some blood? Am I a little girl, that I'm afraid of blood?'

'I didn't say that.'

He nicked himself again. More blood mixed with the white lather.

'Keep in mind. . . *nobody* shaves Irving Kasha, nobody.'

The limousine came to pick us up. 'I'd rather die in Brooklyn,' my father said, as we drove up to JFK.

'You're not dying,' I told him, repeating my assurances as we boarded the plane.

My palpitations had already begun by the time the doors of the DC10 closed. Turning to the stewardess I said anxiously, 'Maybe we can take a later flight.'

She looked bewildered. 'Sir, the pilot's been given the signal for take-off.'

Trapped.

'I'm cold,' my father cried. 'I'm freezing cold.'

The stewardess brought him a blanket.

'This tea isn't good.' And then, five minutes later: 'This coffee isn't good.'

'Look how red your father's face is,' my mother said, grasping my arm.

'Rose!' he screamed. 'I have a pain in my chest. A terrible pain.'

I clung to my composure as the stewardess slipped an oxygen mask over my father's face.

'He's going to die. My husband's going to die. Oh, God, help me, my pressure, my pressure!'

As always in an emergency, my mother made things worse by bearing down on the tragic aspects of the situation. Milking it, turning it into hysteria.

'Irving, Irving. My Irving!'

Again, as I had done before when in the throes of a panic attack on a plane, I took refuge in the toilets. The claustrophobic walls, the miniature sink and toilet, seemed smaller than ever now.

When I returned, I saw they were still driving the stewardess crazy with their histrionics, their demands. My father's illness was pathetically genuine, yet I knew his querulous, childish behaviour would have been the same no matter what state of health he was in.

*I'm going to die before he does*, I thought, returning to the toilets. My presence of mind was fading. This fear wasn't normal; it was a paralysing, all-consuming terror. Every symptom of the past—headaches, lump in the throat, heart skipping beats—descended with crushing impact. *I'm having a nervous breakdown*, I realised. *And I didn't know it. I wouldn't face it.*

The DC 10 hit an air pocket and dropped hundreds of feet.

*He's going to die, he's going to die.* My mother's words hammered at my eardrums, and then I realised it was someone knocking on the toilet door. I had been closeted there for fifteen minutes.

Always locked away, in one cupboard or another.

Maybe I could die first.

It seemed simpler to die than to face the months that lay ahead.

Miraculously, I kept working. Joel and I composed a theme song for Ronald Reagan's 1976 presidential campaign at the request of record executive Mike Curb. Mike later became lieutenant governor of California. He was brilliant, imaginative and—most crucially, since it gave us a basic characteristic in common—a tireless worker.

Record producer and writer Michael Lloyd, who worked with Curb, was another non-stop perfectionist who became a friend and collaborator. Michael, Joel and I launched a productive, consistent partnership in the mid-1970s. A country hit, 'Charlie, I Love Your Wife', resulted immediately from our teamwork.

I was grateful to Curb and Michael Lloyd for their belief in me and their friendship, especially during the months of my father's final deterioration. Meeting Governor Reagan the night our song was performed, and introducing him before a black-tie audience at the Coconut Grove, offered a temporary feeling of optimism.

This optimism was reinforced when he said, 'Thank you for your music,' and commented specifically on the lyrics. He had really listened to every word. He shook my hand with genuine warmth.

I thought of that handshake and the hope it conveyed when listening to my father complain, 'What kind of doctors are those? Why can't they give me something for the pain?'

*Be sympathetic. He's suffering.*

'Let Ceil cook for me. . . don't let your mother cook,' he said once. 'Always hated her lousy cooking anyway.'

My father didn't let up:

'Your brother doesn't even call.'

'Your mother wishes I would die.'

'You all want me to die.'

'You're not dying,' I said automatically, as he lost weight and his skin turned a sallow, yellowish colour.

My mother flew back to Brooklyn to collect the rest of her belongings, close all bank accounts and sell the shop. On the day of her return, Joel and I were well into a book on songwriting, *If They Ask You, You Can Write a Song*, and Ceil volunteered to pick her up at the airport. After Ceil left the room, my father said, 'You go and pick up your mother.'

'But Ceil's going.'

'Alfred, it's not right. You can't let the *shiksa* go.'

'What do you mean?'

'I mean, she's not family. She shouldn't go to the airport. You should go.'

I couldn't believe it. He was living in my house, receiving care and attention that amounted to professional nursing from my wife, and he was still saying 'the *shiksa*'.

I didn't argue; he was clearly dying.

Without explaining the reason to Ceil, I told her I would collect my mother. She was waiting, suitcases on either side of her. In her chubby hand was a large blue bag. I reached for it.

'No, I'll carry the bag myself.'

'What's in it?'

'Nothing. Papers.'

'What kind of papers?'

'Papers. Does it matter?'

'I just wondered. Is it a secret?'

'No.' But she clutched the bag tighter.

'You know, Ceil was going to come and pick you up, but Daddy said, "Don't let the *shiksa* go; *you* pick Mother up."'

Without the slightest pause, she answered, 'He's right. You're my son, you should be the one to come.'

'Not the *shiksa*.'

'That's right.'

'She's not family, right?'

'Look, Ceil is a nice girl.'

'A nice girl.'

'But you're my son.'

I reached again for the blue bag. 'That's heavy. Let me carry it.'

'No.'

I grabbed the bag from her hands.

'I want to carry it. Give it back.' Alarm creased her features. Animal fear.

'What's in it?'

'Give it back or I'll call the police.'

'Call the police? You'd call the police on your son?'

She lunged for the bag. I held it out of her grasp.

'Police! Police!'

Horrified, I let her have the blue bag back. We fought all the way home; motorway traffic doubled the normal length of the drive.

We arrived at the house, and my mother leapt from the car and ran inside. I followed her, not unloading the cases.

'I want to see what's in that bag,' I demanded.

'It's mine.'

It occurred to me, for the first time, that my mother had never backed down from anything; never admitted she was wrong, never yielded one point in an argument. Though round and fleshy, her jaw had a tight, determined quality. Her eyes never smiled, even when her lips did.

'Rose, what's happening?' My father's breath-starved voice distracted her. In that instant, I took the blue bag and ran into my room, slamming the door behind me and locking it. Something told me that I had to know; that the key to comprehending my life lay in that bag. I hardly heard the pounding on the door. Hypnotised, I unzipped the bag and stared at its contents as they poured onto my bed.

Wealth—stocks, bonds, cash, cheque books from a dozen different banks—tumbled out. One hundred, two hundred thousand dollars, and then I stopped counting. How could I reconcile this hidden wealth with the sordid circumstances of my early life? My mother's phrase, 'We can't afford it,' rang discordantly in my mind.

'We can't afford a bed for you *and* Larry.'

'We can't afford clothes for you *and* Larry.'

'We can't afford a holiday.'

'We can't afford to give you money for the cinema.'

And all the time, she was piling up a hidden fortune—money pocketed from the till when my father was too drunk to notice.

I opened the door and she fell upon the bed, gathering up her treasure, incoherently screeching and cursing, a wild-eyed female Scrooge. Totally exposed. The worst of it was my realisation that she felt no embarrassment or guilt—only rage that she had been found out; that her treasure might be torn away.

'Did you think I'd steal it if I knew?' I asked her. 'Do you think Ceil and I need your filthy money? I can make my own money. . . .' and I rattled on and on, trying to bring my outrage under control by shouting it into submission.

'It's mine!' my mother sobbed. 'Mine and your father's, for our old age. Our old age.'

Enraged as I was, I couldn't say the cruellest words of all: *Your old age? What old age? Your husband is a dead man. He can hardly move. Your old age alone, you mean. Your old age. Only yours.*

In the days ahead, my mother struggled to smooth over the disagreement.

'I was saving it for you—for you and Larry.'

'I was saving it for Dana, for my granddaughter, so she could have the best. For Dana, darling, for Dana.'

As my father disintegrated, Joel and I were exposed, by

contrast, to a lighter, more fanciful world—the world of Disney. For five years we had had meetings with story editor Frank Paris. Frank had repeatedly told us: 'Disney will do a musical, but only if it's a classic. It has to be a classic.'

We were finally given the go-ahead on a project, an original called *Pete's Dragon*, conceived in the 1920s by Walt Disney himself. My dream of a full movie musical had come true. We were told to write twelve songs for the film, which would combine live action and animation.

The sense of cheerful unreality was heightened by our surroundings: Mickey Avenue, Dopey Drive. Our little office had posters of Donald Duck, the Love Bug and Snow White. Everyone on the premises was friendly; it was a shiny world of Doris Day smiles and spontaneous handshakes. A world that said, 'You can have problems, but don't bring them to the studio.'

Our old friend Irwin Kostal did the arrangements, and the casting of *The Poseidon Adventure* friends Red Buttons and Shelley Winters made for a family-type atmosphere. Mickey Rooney and Jim Dale were cast quickly. All we lacked was a leading lady.

Helen Reddy wanted the part. The company's first choice was Olivia Newton-John but she was unavailable. Joel and I recommended Helen to head of production Ron Miller.

'Put in a good word for me,' Helen urged whenever we saw her. She won the role after a natural and assured screen test.

Red, Jim and Helen displayed consistent good humour. Shelley was outstanding as Pete's wicked stepmother, though she created as much drama off set as on. They called me at 2.00am, requesting lyric changes for a 9.00am recording session. She came on the set in a wheelchair to protest choreography she considered too acrobatic.

I remembered a Bette Davis quote, in which she claimed that people had to fight for perfection, even if it created temporary turmoil. In the end, Shelley was brilliant, and I understood the integrity that had directed her behaviour.

I thought of Henry Fonda, in that small Oregon motel, doing 300 spots, investing heart and soul in a tedious but necessary job. That memory helped. It reminded me of the essential quality pros need: a willingness to stretch, to test new things, to think of the whole picture.

Love can flow from creative interaction, but it isn't the main point, only a happy by-product in certain instances. One instance where it did happen was when I became friendly with an actor in the film named Gary Morgan. Gary played Shelley Winters' son, the younger of two evil brothers (Jeff Conaway of *Taxi* was the other). Gary was an acrobat, slim and muscular, with a leprechaun smile. He was also a Jew who believed in Christ. I couldn't help notice the parallels. On *The Poseidon Adventure* set, I had met Mark, the first man to share his spiritual feelings with me. Shelley Winters and Red Buttons had both been in that film. Now Shelley and Red were working with me again, and another young man, similar in size and build to Mark, was talking about his faith.

'I've never been happier,' Gary said, executing a cartwheel.

'You don't seem religious.'

'Why? What's "religious" supposed to be?' He pulled a long face. 'Serious. . . grim. . . full of authority? Rubbish! I have fun. I love my wife and two kids and my ten animals (among them four monkeys and two snakes). But I love God too.'

Gary hugged me before going back to work on a scene. 'You'll find out one of these days.'

'Maybe.'

He winked. 'You think I'm a little *meshugenah* for a Christian? Hey, I'm Jewish. . . I'm a Jew who believes in Jesus.'

'When was the last time you had a salami sandwich

and cream soda?'

    'Last night. At Cantors. Just before I went to church.'

    'Gary, you're having me on.'

    'I'm not,' he said, with unexpected intensity. 'You'll find out.'

# 14

# *Escaping the Darkness*

The film was into its final days of shooting when my parents announced they were returning to New York.

'I said I'll die in Brooklyn, and I will,' my father insisted.

The morning he left I watched him shaving. The razor hung loosely in his fingers; he was so weak that even a razor qualified as a heavy object.

'Alfred,' he whispered. 'Shave me.'

Those were words I had never expected to hear. I had to hear him say the phrase twice before I could act on it.

'Shave me, Alfred. Shave me, son.'

I took the razor—a straight razor, the one he had used when he was active as a barber—and carefully grazed his face. The skin seemed like paper; I had a feeling it would strip off, layer by layer, when confronted with a blade. But I went on, watching the tears he had at last allowed to fall.

'Thank you, son.' His gnarled right hand touched my cheek. 'I love you, son.'

'I love you too.'

A month later he died, on Avenue M. Right above the shop where he had been a barber for forty-five years.

I didn't fly back East. By now my agoraphobia was totally paralysing. I didn't drive, or take a train, or go near an airport. Even travelling to Disney was accomplished through the aid of tranquillisers, and Joel always drove.

Ceil and Larry flew to the funeral without me. Later on, Ceil called and described a macabre moment when my

144

mother threw herself on the coffin and cried, 'Irving, Irving, how could you leave me in the prime of our lives?'

Was any shred of her grief genuine, or was she simply surrendering to her tendency for self-dramatisation? According to Ceil, onlookers blanched at this display, knowing how much my mother had hated her husband for over forty-five years. Hated him enough to corner Joel at a party and say, 'Your wife is a lucky woman to have such a nice man. I wasn't so lucky. But there was a man, a Mr Klinger. He was a pharmacist. . .'

Nevertheless, the simple act of sharing, of close proximity, creates bonds, no matter how neurotic these bonds may appear to other people. Part of her must have suffered; part of her must have felt abandoned. The known, even if painful, is preferable to the unknown when human beings are basically fearful. And my mother, for all her talk, was a frightened person.

I had to ask myself: Larry and I could have supported her. She could, in fact, have supported herself. Why didn't she ever leave him?

I prayed that one day I'd find the answer.

Tragedy replaced tragedy, making it impossible for Ceil and me to recover from the pressure of living with my parents and the shock of my father's death. Ceil's mother and father—both ill, respectively, with cancer and the aftermath of a stroke—died within three months of each other in 1977. The horror of visiting graves became an almost routine occurrence.

Suddenly Ceil felt lost, cut loose from childhood securities. She needed my strength and I was psychologically unable to supply it.

There's a point, experts now recognise, when the nerve endings in certain people are physically burned down— like defective wires. I was one of those people. It was nearly impossible for me to get up in the morning. I had no energy. Eating was a chore. Working, once the prime passion of my life, was back-breaking effort that yielded no satisfaction.

Joel and I continued to write music for Disney: 'Freaky Friday', 'Hot Lead and Cold Feet' and 'The North Avenue Irregulars'. We felt, more than ever, that we had found our niche with family films. I couldn't help noticing a review written about the 1979 sci-fi hit *Alien*, in which a critic said, 'Stomach-churning violence, slime and shocks.' It seemed to me that stomach-churning violence was becoming a mandatory part of most Hollywood films, and the trend was far from healthy.

Children were our greatest future resource, and it was irresponsible to offer only a warped, bleak view of the world. When I said these things, I was accused of being old fashioned.

Only Disney resisted this trend, and I admired them for it. But much as I liked being at Disney studios, Joel and I did all our writing at my home. If our presence had been required daily on the premises, I would have given up these jobs.

When I turned forty, I told friends that it didn't bother me. 'I don't feel any different,' I said. A burst of youthful energy carried me through the first few months. I played basketball in my backyard, swam vigorously at eight every morning, did push-ups, read a whole stack of books I had been meaning to get to. And collapsed.

Dying became an obsession. The idea that I hadn't gone far enough, that my goals were still unachieved, haunted me. I read an article in the *L.A. Times* about 'boy geniuses' and decided I was over the hill; it was too late to write all the books, shows and songs I wanted to write.

Leaving the house, even to walk around the corner, became virtually impossible. Nor did I welcome the presence of people. One Saturday night Ceil invited a group of fourteen for dinner, and I ordered her to cancel it—an hour before guests were scheduled to arrive.

In a panic, intimidated by my hostility, she rushed to the phone and managed to stop guests who were halfway through the front doors of their homes.

Ceil formed a habit of covering up for me. 'He's not feeling well. . . Dana's sick. . . we're too tired. . .' became automatic responses. She erected a life pattern around my neuroses and fears.

Suppressing rage—not an easy thing for Ceil, who is direct and spontaneously emotional—resulted in headaches and fits of crying. Little irritations, like a misplaced bill or an unreturned phone call, provoked a flood of tears. Through it all, she fought to be strong and supportive; to reassure me that everything would be all right.

She tried to treat my illness as though it were just a phase, a period of temporary insanity. Cancelled plans, delayed meals were 'no big deal'.

'Is it my fault?' she would ask me. 'Something I've done?'

I assured her it wasn't.

Only after I hid from guests we had invited over, and refused to come downstairs to greet them, did Ceil acknowledge the severity of my condition.

'Al, what's wrong?' she asked, with undisguised horror in her eyes.

'I don't know,' I told her. 'I just. . . couldn't face having them here.'

It was inevitable, given the accumulation of differences, that our marriage would suffer. We clashed when Joel and I were offered a film in England and I turned it down.

'It's a terrific script,' Ceil said. (I always gave her my scripts to read for her opinion.) 'It has a good cast. They're spending a lot of money to plug it.'

'We have plenty to do right here in California,' I answered feebly.

'What are you doing? You've worked twenty-five years

to build up a reputation in this business. Are you going to throw it away now?'

'It's too far.... Dana needs me.... The money's not good enough. . . .' I made every conceivable excuse.

'You can't just hang around the house,' Ceil said. And then: 'Maybe you should see a doctor again.'

'By doctor you mean psychiatrist?'

'Yes.'

'I don't need a psychiatrist. I just need to rest for a while. . . stay at home and rest.'

I pursued projects when the meetings could be held at my home. Elia Kazan and Budd Schulberg came to talk about a musical version of *A Face in the Crowd*. They agreed to work with us if money could be raised.

Larry volunteered to raise the needed capital. He didn't get financing for *A Face in the Crowd*, but he did find backers for a stage version of the old MGM classic *Seven Brides for Seven Brothers*. He asked us to write eight songs for the new Broadway-bound version, and signed Jane Powell and Howard Keel to repeat their original film parts. My anxieties descended on me: How could I go to a theatre every day for rehearsals. . . fly to out-of-town openings. . . meet at the homes of writers, choreographers?

My brother persuaded me to get involved. He sensed my emotional difficulties and told me to relax, not to worry.

'I'm always here for you,' he said, in a sentimental, half-embarrassed voice. Then he hugged me.

I clung to that memory. My brother had never been physically demonstrative before.

Age and experience helped our relationship. So did the passing away of my father. My parents had always been a dividing force and even the absence of one made our communication more comfortable. My mother still resorted to old tactics: 'Larry called me today and you didn't,' or, 'Alfred got me a birthday present. Why didn't you?' But her efforts had less impact. An artistic barrier had also been knocked down. Larry had been impressed with *Pete's Dragon*, and felt that the song 'Candle on the Water' and score (which were both nominated for Oscars), indicated a flair for Broadway writing.

*Seven Brides* opened in Dallas to triumphant reviews and the best box office that city had ever seen.

'You should be happy,' Ceil said.

'I am.'

'Can we fly to Dallas to see it?'

'No.'


At last I acknowledged that the problems were too deep-seated to handle alone. Battles between Ceil and me were increasing; I was neglecting my daughter.

Symptoms ran my life: palpitations before every professional meeting; hyperventilating the few times I stepped into a car; headaches.

I refused to enter department stores, even when Ceil was with me. I couldn't finish a meal in a restaurant. I had to dash out abruptly, sometimes after the first few minutes; sometimes in the middle of a meal.

Holidays were out.

Flying was out.

An attempt to defeat the flying phobia was disastrous. Ceil and I had planned a trip to New York. We made it to Los Angeles International Airport and checked in our luggage. So far, so good.

'It'll be fine. You wait and see,' Ceil promised.

'Flight 23 is boarding,' came the announcement.

I reached the entrance, where the stewardess was inspecting boarding passes.

My stomach started to swim; instant nausea made me double over. The attack hit with sudden, disabling force. I heard myself groan.

'I can't go on the flight,' I said to Ceil.

I stepped aside and sat down. My hands were stretched

out, as though to grab something, but there was nothing but space.

'Last call for Flight 23. . . .'

I heard my father's voice, on our flight from Brooklyn to Los Angeles just before he died: 'Rose! I have a pain in my chest, a terrible pain.' And my mother's response: 'He's going to die. My husband's going to die. Oh, God, help me, my pressure, my pressure.'

'Please try to get on,' pleaded Ceil. 'I'll be with you. You can listen to music through the earphones, or watch a film, or just sleep. It'll be over in no time.'

*Why didn't she understand*, I wondered, *that boarding Flight 23 was certain death?* I saw the bewildered faces of airline personnel, asking Ceil what they could do to help. I sensed Ceil's hopelessness when she shook her head and muttered, 'Nothing.'

Flight 23 arrived safely at JFK six hours later. Our luggage took the trip alone.

It was simpler, after a while, to stay in bed as long as possible. Joel had recently rented an office, with the hope of coaxing me from the house. I had agreed, not believing it would do any good. Morning after morning Joel called and said, 'I'm here. When are you coming over?'

'I don't know if I can make it,' was my standard response.

'You've got to get out of the house.'

'I'll be there at 10.30.'

Ten-thirty came and Joel would call again. 'Do you want me to come and pick you up?'

'No, I. . . why don't we work here?'

'We have this office, and there'll be no distractions. We can get more done.'

'Tomorrow, then.'

Tomorrow repeated the same pattern. Joel hid his impatience. He realised I had a serious problem. But the cat-and-mouse game of will-you-or-won't-you-come-to-the-office? eventually proved too much for us. We surrendered the office to another tenant.

Pressure escalated. We were in the midst of building a new pool, and a constant drilling noise scraped away at my eardrums. I wanted to scream: 'Stop it! The noise is driving me crazy!' Instead I buried my head in a pillow, as my teeth ground into my lips and drew blood.

The noise stopped when our pool company went bankrupt. Ceil had to handle the nightmare of a lawsuit.

'I can't do this alone,' she would cry. I was helpless to ease her burdens. Our roles had reversed. I had always been the parent, taken care of every problem in my life. Now I felt unequal to the simplest responsibility.

Ceil kept on at me until I took a tentative step towards getting well. Friends recommended a licensed marriage, family and child counsellor named Maralyn Teare. She was a bright, sympathetic young woman who helped identify my inexplicable terrors. Maralyn, fortunately, was willing to come to my home. She understood how thoroughly agoraphobia could paralyse a patient's movements.

'There are agoraphobics,' she told me, 'who haven't left their areas of security for thirty or forty years.'

I recalled the publisher Carl, in New York, and his wife. The woman everyone had laughed at—the phantom, the shadow—the poor soul who had been incapable of leaving her home.

'I thought only women had agoraphobia,' I said.

'Just as many men have this problem as women,' said Maralyn, 'but men have a greater stake in concealing it. The fear makes them feel weak, unmasculine. The fact that so many men suffer from agoraphobia is often forgotten.'

*The forgotten agoraphobic*, I thought.

'All I need,' I told Maralyn, 'is something to help me sleep.'

'It's not as simple as that.'

I plunged ahead. 'Then, if I can get some rest, I can find the energy to fight this thing!'

'That's just what you shouldn't do,' Maralyn said. 'You don't fight agoraphobia; you don't conquer it with will power. That's what you've been trying to do—beat it back with sheer will.'

I stayed focused; I wanted a pill that would supply a miraculous answer. Pills, Maralyn felt, were a stop-gap solution, although there were anti-depressants that offered relief to agoraphobics.

The next time I saw Maralyn, I opened up more.

'I never used to be like this,' I told her. 'I jumped on a plane at a moment's notice. I was game for anything.'

'Many agoraphobics lead normal lives—and then suddenly become paralysed.'

'What am I afraid of?'

'Well, for one thing, losing control.' She went on to say that agoraphobics, being perfectionists, dread making fools of themselves. After a few humiliating episodes they develop a fear of revealing their panic and inadequacy before strangers. Ultimately, they hide at home so that their loss of composure won't occur publicly.

'Maybe,' Maralyn suggested, 'you put exaggerated importance on what people think. Approval matters too much. You're afraid. . . .'

'I'm not afraid,' I said automatically, though I had just used the word myself. I didn't like the sound of it from someone else's lips, even though my life was being ruled by fear. 'And as far as caring what people think is concerned, I don't need them. If my work is going well, everything's fine.'

'Really? It seems as though your work is going well now.' After a pause, she added, 'You've got to learn that everyone is afraid. And people, particularly phobics, feel isolated, as though their difficulties are happening only to them. You have to let your friends and family know so they can help. You need positive reinforcement.'

I took refuge in wordplay. 'That's an analyst's phrase—"positive reinforcement".'

She didn't let the jibe intimidate her. 'There are relaxation exercises you should do.'

I listened politely, unconvinced.

'Exercises where you visualise. Close your eyes and think of a calm blue ocean, a long stretch of desert, a sunset. If you have a pet you might concentrate on the pet. Many pet owners find their animals more soothing than any other image.' That was the first suggestion that strongly registered with me. I had a cat, Snow, that I loved. Snow slept with Ceil and me, and his motionless white body, curled up on the edge of our bed, had always struck me as the essence of tranquillity.

'Once the body is relaxed,' Maralyn continued, 'the mind will follow suit. The trouble is, so many of us concentrate (what amounts to negative meditation) on all the things that can go wrong, the things that worry us. Positive imagery can counteract that.'

Alone in my room, I did as she said. I found my mind resisting all efforts to be calm. My brain was like a piece of jerky, unedited film. As soon as a positive image flashed on, the film shook and blacked out, and negative thoughts overran it. I became fidgety, or I began to itch. My toes wiggled, or I would feel a need to clear my throat.

'It takes time,' Maralyn said. 'Of course your negative impulses will put up a fight. But concentration will win out.'

Maybe I wasn't trying hard enough, or I just didn't fully accept her suggestions, much as I wanted to. I also tried to eat properly. Maralyn stressed proper nutrition, attempting to wean me from coffee and products containing caffeine, which caused excitability and lowered my blood sugar. She urged me to reduce my sugar intake too.

'I want to get better,' I told her. 'I want to move around freely again.'

'You will. I promise.'

Her influence was important, because it offered the first stirrings of insight. More insight followed when she brought up a nationally known course TERRAP (Territorial Apprehension), which dealt exclusively with the symptoms of phobic illness. This highly effective course, which claimed a cure rate of eighty per cent, was the creation of Dr Arthur Hardy of Menlo Park, California. I saw Dr Hardy for a sixty-minute interview and felt TERRAP might be the answer.

Like Maralyn, Dr Hardy preferred a therapeutic approach to the steady use of anti-depressant drugs like Imipramine and Amitriptyline, or anti-anxiety drugs like Valium.

The first night Ceil drove me to a TERRAP meeting, it took superhuman effort to leave the house. My fear was compounded by a reluctance to attend the meeting and risk possible exposure. I thought: *Industry people might see me. They'll think I'm a weakling and say to themselves, 'He's unreliable, an employment risk; look how far down he's gone.'*

This particular group met in the cellar of a two-storey house in Cheviot Hills. The descent down a narrow staircase to the basement aggravated my claustrophobia. There were fourteen people present that evening: twelve women and two men. The other man was heavy-set, with grey hair and old-fashioned horn-rimmed glasses. His expression reflected the embarrassment I felt. I was also ashamed of being a minority male in a roomful of females.

I wondered how I could be suffering from such a feminine disease.

A woman named Elaine Garwood conducted the meeting, flanked by two assistants. All were agoraphobics.

I looked around quickly, to make certain nobody I knew was in the room. I watched as Elaine scribbled 'Agoraphobia' on a blackboard.

'How many of you have felt an attack spring out of

nowhere?' she asked. There were nods and raised hands. Tentatively I raised mine.

All the physical symptoms Elaine described—the palpitations, fainting spells, drenched palms—were familiar to me. But she didn't shrug off the seriousness of a pounding heart.

'It's probably anxiety,' she said. 'Most of you will find there's nothing physically wrong; but just to be sure, go for a check-up. Make sure you're physically OK, and after you've had a check-up, you can start exercising. Exercise is one of the best ways of releasing tension and repressed hostility.' She recommended visualisation, like Maralyn, as well as relaxation tapes, and advised us to dictate our own suggestions into a machine. 'Your own voice is often more effective than the voice of a stranger,' she said. 'Also, keep a diary. It will help you to unburden yourself and enable you to see how you're progressing.'

Her advice made perfect sense, but I found myself wondering when the meeting would be over. I kept staring at my watch.

Elaine talked about sharing our problems; feeling a sense of community. None of her words pierced my loneliness.

'I can't stand it any more!' A violent, male voice sheared through my self-preoccupation. 'I'm a prisoner in my own home because of my wife. We never go on holiday, we never even go to a show. And what's worse, she resents it when I go out. What the hell am I supposed to do?'

His wife, a tiny mid-fortyish blonde, exploded into tears.

'I do want to go on holiday,' she sobbed.

'You don't, or you'd make more of an effort. You'd try harder.'

'I am trying,' she screamed. 'I'm trying as hard as I can.'

Elaine calmed the outraged husband down, reiterating what Maralyn had said to me: phobic fears could not be banished by will power alone.

After that the stories began flowing. An angry wife ridiculed her husband for his inability to sign his own credit card. 'It's just plain stupid to have a fear like that,' she said. Her face was red; I could feel she was at the end of her rope. 'Is the credit card going to bite him? It doesn't make sense.'

'Maybe it makes sense if he had a bad experience in a bank when he was younger,' Elaine pointed out.

The husband remained silent, resistant; his gaze shifted to the door.

Elaine waited, sensing his indecision.

'When I was a kid,' the man said, without preparation, 'my mum and I went to withdraw some money. She handed over the slip after filling it out, and the cashier. . . .'

'Go on,' Elaine said.

'He handed it back to her and said, "There's no money here. Your husband withdrew it earlier today." And my mother went crazy. She yelled at the cashier and said it was impossible, he should check again, but he shook his head. It was a terrible scene, and they had to drag her away. Everybody was watching us, staring, thinking, "Who's this crazy lady? The woman has lost her mind." She cried all the way home and all the next day. My dad had left town with the money.' He cleared his throat. 'He never came back.'

'Oh, my goodness,' said Ceil.

'That was twenty, thirty years ago,' the man's wife said.

'Yes,' said Elaine. 'But certain memories. . . certain events that formed us. . . stay alive. They're as alive to us as the day they happened.'

I studied Ceil. She loved me, and she had been supportive during my illness. But I knew she identified with the pain the man's wife was suffering. I knew agoraphobia was bewildering to her. It seemed so simple, from her point of view, to stand in line at a bank or take a lift, let alone step out of the house. At the next meeting we attended, she had the courage to admit before the group, 'I love Al... but sometimes I just don't understand.' Sympathetic murmurs followed her statement. It was cathartic for her to let her long-hidden feelings show. In a burst of emotion she pleaded, 'Al's in such pain. Help him. Please help my husband!'

If I had ever thought I was alone in my agoraphobic world, I learned otherwise after statistics of the disease were revealed. According to the National Institute of Mental Health, one adult in every twenty suffers from it. Forty per cent of phobics, Elaine said, had relatives with the same malady.

We learned further variations of visualisation. Members were desensitised by exercises in which they imagined themselves trapped in frightening situations for increasing periods of time.

'Once you actually imagine yourself being in a plane or a supermarket or bank for fifteen minutes without fear, you can actually be in it,' said a TERRAP counsellor. 'At first you'll experience every symptom of terror, because the brain literally cannot distinguish between an image clearly visualised and a real event. But take comfort, your body can't sustain a high level of panic indefinitely, and if the phobic can be induced simply to endure the thing he feels long enough, his anxiety will wear off and he can often be cured at once.'

*Why can't I accept all this?* I asked myself desperately. *It makes sense, but something in me keeps battling it.*

The family pool remained unfinished, and this seemingly insignificant difficulty mushroomed into a life-and-death issue. Ceil and I tried to avoid attacking each other directly by venting our rage on the progress of the lawsuit.

'You're not behind me,' I would say accusingly. 'You're not supportive.'

'I've done everything I can do.'

'I'm always there for people and no one is there for me,' I ranted. 'It's time somebody took care of me.'

The charge was so unjust, so outrageous, in view of Ceil's loving efforts, that she wouldn't answer. She couldn't even cry. I watched her swallow; watched her face darken.

'You're just like my mother,' I said. 'It's Rose Kasha all over again.'

Anger that had gone underground, anger crushed under the merciless weight of my mother's, 'Be nice,' was gushing to the surface, threatening to tear apart the fabric of my life.

I chastised myself for being selfish. Why couldn't I appreciate what God had given me? So many blessings had come my way. I counted them daily. I observed other people less fortunate and gained increasing awareness of my good fortune.

Nothing lifted the depression.

Finally I couldn't cope with it any more. Ceil and I were both exhausted from endless fighting. Our self-images were torn, bleeding. Neither of us could handle the sense of failure, the anger and disappointment flying in all directions. We could not possibly sort out our tangled emotions in a climate of twenty-four-hour togetherness.

'I want you to leave,' Ceil said one night. 'I can't stand this any more.'

She was crying as she packed my suitcase. 'Not everything is my fault.'

'I didn't say it was.'

'I need some time alone. We both do. I can't see where I'm going. You've given up on the TERRAP meetings. You won't see a psychiatrist. You won't help yourself . . . so how can I help you?'

'Nobody can help me.'

I spent that night, and the next three weeks, in a friend's flat. Joel called often and filled me in on our work developments. *If They Ask You, You Can Write a Song*, the book we'd written on composing, had come out and received good reviews. *Seven Brides* was scheduled to open at the Dorothy Chandler Pavilion in Los Angeles.

'Maybe you'll come to the opening,' Joel said. 'If you're feeling better.'

'I'll see,' I said, knowing I was emotionally incapable of mingling with crowds.

It was three in the morning. I couldn't sleep. I resisted the urge to take a Valium or a Melloril. I had decided to kick the pills by myself; to straighten out my life without the aid of a therapist. A week before, in a fit of self-reproach about my 'weakness', I had stopped seeing Maralyn Teare.

Maralyn had warned me, 'You can't do this with will power. It's not that simple.' I didn't believe her. Determination had always served me well before.

'Conscious fighting,' she said, 'only aggravates the tension. The trick is to accept your symptoms and anxieties as they appear, and just float.'

The passivity she advocated was just too far removed from my natural inclinations. I had always thought I could control my fate by tightening my grip on it. As a result I had never trusted anyone to take responsibility. Unless I did it, it would never get done, or if done, it would be incorrectly executed. No matter how competently Ceil and Joel did a job, I worried every time a new challenge presented itself, unless it remained under my surveillance and supervision.

My palpitations were worse than ever. Despite Maralyn's assurance that they were harmless, I knew deep down that they were forerunners of a heart attack. How long, after all, could my body accept such constant punishment?

Despair filled me; despair so total that it exceeded grief. The despair stemmed from utter hopelessness. I heard myself moan, and the moaning built into a gasp, then a sob, then tears poured out. My body trembled, and the tears splashed from my eyes and down my face. I tasted those bitter drops on my tongue and the crying grew wilder, more desperate.

'God, if you're listening, help me,' I said. As I said it, I couldn't help feeling I had made a mess of everything. I didn't deserve God's love. Nevertheless, I ached for it.

I stared at the ceiling, the floor, the window. Loneliness blocked me in every direction.

I reached for the television dial, as though it were a life preserver, and a fuzzy picture flashed on. I wiped away the tears and saw Reverend Robert Schuller.

It was a replay of an old Schuller broadcast on Trinity Broadcasting.

What was he saying? I struggled to hear. It seemed vital to make out the words.

'Perfect love casts out all fear.'

Big deal. How simplistic. I loved my wife and daughter. I loved my friends. I loved my work. What good did it do?

'Love casts out all fear.'

And then, automatically, I reversed it.

'Fear casts out all love.'

How much had I really loved anyone this past year? Wasn't the poison of bitterness my overriding emotion? Hadn't I become so fixated on resenting my parents and the old hurts of childhood that these hurts had finally taken precedence over any affection? Had I really failed to make the transition from my first family to my second, as Ceil had said?

'Fear casts out all love.'

I had been afraid. Twenty-four hours a day, running in circles of fear, the fear growing every minute. Afraid of failing everybody—Ceil, Dana, Joel, my parents, the artists I worked with, the friends I had made. Until it became easier to imprison myself behind phobias, to hide from the world.

I sensed, without quite knowing how to articulate it, that my only answer was in getting off myself, tearing the focus from my own psyche and soul and transferring it. Self-analysis had been self-abuse.

'If you put your trust in God, you'll find more peace than you've ever known.'

I didn't have to take on all responsibility. I didn't have to strive for perfection; I only had to be real. Nor did I have to punish myself for what I perceived to be monumental failures. No human being was perfect; only God was. And all he asked of me, I suddenly realised, was to do my best. Through Reverend Schuller, he was telling me I could, at last, forgive myself.

'Jesus.' I uttered the word hesitantly. Fear diminished and I kept saying the name, again and again, feeling my agony of spirit subside with every repetition.

And then, I had a sense that a blinding light was filling the room. It seemed to me that a window had opened. Whether the window of my soul, or an actual window, I've never been quite sure. But there was an opening, a healing, a flowering inside that flooded my heart.

The tears had stopped; the end of a sudden summer shower. I had no urge to cry any more. I left the television on. Reverend Schuller's voice gave me a childlike security, and I closed my eyes.

Without the crutch of Valium or any other pill, I fell asleep.

The next morning I drove home to see Dana and Ceil. I didn't have to call Ceil and ask her to pick me up. I got into my car, waiting for symptoms, and was shocked at their absence. Peace washed over me. A peace all the more powerful for its stillness. Unthinkingly I shouted with joy, and then began to laugh. The laughter became uncontrollable and I went with it, letting it sweep me up. The laughter was totally devoid of self-consciousness. It wouldn't have mattered if people looked through the window and wondered what madman was laughing all by himself. The old how-are-my-actions-affecting-people? apparatus was, blessedly, failing to operate.

When I arrived home I hugged Ceil and Dana with pent-up feeling. I couldn't bear to let them go.

Ceil and I went for a short walk, and she said casually, 'Pat Hollis came round yesterday.' Pat was a friend of ours, a peformer who sang for a Christian record label. Ceil's casual tone changed. 'She and I went to church.'

I didn't answer, didn't breathe. I thought of Reverend Schuller; of my devastating, life-changing experience.

Pat called that afternoon, and suggested we all go to church the following morning. We did, and the visit was so inspiring and soothing that we went the next week, and the week after. I felt as though all demons had been put to rest—till tremors of anxiety rocked me during a service.

*Hold on. Don't fight. Don't tense up. Float with it.*

'Are you all right?' Ceil asked, squeezing my hand.

'Yes.'

A few minutes later I was. I looked up at the sunny stained-glass ceiling of the church and offered thanks.

Ceil was thrilled by my change, but guarded. 'Do you want to go a meeting?' she asked occasionally. We did, in fact, go to an occasional group session designed to help phobics, and I usually drove there. There were moments when I longed for Ceil to take over, but I fought the feeling down. I had read an excerpt of a sermon by Jack Hayford, Pastor of Church on the Way. Hayford had talked about the importance of man's role in marriage and in the home; the necessity for male strength and leadership. I kept reviewing those words as I drove, especially when assailed by that unexpected, out-of-nowhere dread that makes a phobic attack so frightening.

In the beginning I drove slowly, less than twenty miles an hour. Ceil would lean over to help me steer till I gently pushed her hands away. I would park and pray; we both prayed. The spiritual reinforcement steadied my quaking insides. Restarting the engine, I would manage to make it to our destination.

I viewed the meetings differently from before. The total self-involvement, typical of full-blown agoraphobia, had eased, and I gained greater awareness of the suffering experienced by others in a similar predicament. I was able, increasingly, to separate myself; to say, 'That poor man,' rather than, 'Poor me—that's how *I* feel.'

I came to understand that the male was, both in press and public awareness, the forgotten agoraphobic. His painful isolation was ignored. The cliché about male strength made it difficult for men to step foward and admit they were being destroyed by phobic symptoms, and I felt it was my job to let them know they had someone to talk to.

The influence of newfound faith helped me to step beyond my own insecurities, and I took to phoning other phobics, persuading them to share their troubles with me over the phone.

The night before our thirteenth wedding anniversary, Ceil and I lay in bed. 'We came through, somehow,' I said.

'I know. I can't believe it.' She touched my face. 'It's our anniversary tomorrow, and I prayed things would be better by the time it came.'

'Can you ever forgive me?'

She clung tighter.

'You can lean on me,' I said. 'I promise I won't fall. Besides, don't forget we're not alone. We've got a pretty impressive helper on our side.'

'I didn't forget.'

'We both have to remember—and keep remembering. How can you stumble when God is with you? And how can I stumble, ever again, if you're with me?'

Ceil turned away. Compliments embarrassed her.

'Honey, you're everything to me. That's what God made

me see most of all.'

'You're so corny, do you know that?'

'Yes. When it comes to you, I'm corny. Listen, I have an idea.' I took her face in my hands. 'Ceil, will you marry me?'

'I'm already married, dear.'

'I mean it. Let's get married again. Let's really start afresh.'

'That's crazy, isn't it?'

'Maybe. So what? It's our chance to make a new . . . a new morning after for ourselves. What do you say?'

She clapped her hands together. 'I love the idea. I love the thought of saying our vows again. Just the thought of it makes me feel eighteen years old.'

We held each other without another word, letting our unspoken joy and hope do the talking for us.

Two weeks later we were married in our living room, surrounded by friends. Gabriel Ferrer, son of Jose Ferrer and Rosemary Clooney, and a minister Ceil and I had become friendly with in church, performed the ceremony. Next to him was his soon-to-be-wife, Debby Boone.

Ceil and I kept looking at each other, savouring the miracle. We had never stopped caring for each other, but this was something different—a return to youthful feelings that had been buried under years of pressure.

I was falling in love with my wife all over again.

Discovery is exciting but difficult. Nothing worth gaining comes without effort, and Christianity is no exception. After the first ardent weeks of any love affair, questioning begins.

I was Jewish. Did this mean I had to give up my heritage, my past, everything that had made me who I was?

No matter what path I followed, I knew I would feel a cultural love and connection to Judaism all my life.

*Don't rush it*, I told myself. *A colt walks unsteadily at first, until he develops power in his legs.*

My early spirituality was reinforced when Ceil and I attended a weekly Bible class. Gabriel Ferrer held the classes in his mother's guest house.

I discussed agoraphobia at the class, and everyone was sympathetic and understanding. They prayed for me; for my permanent cure from the disease.

One young man in particular took a gratifyingly personal interest in my symptoms. His name was Clark Mathias, and he had come from Wheaton, Illinois, to manage a car dealership. Clark had a heart as big as his broad 6ft 3in frame. Sandy brown hair and a beard completed the overall impression of a gentle giant. His gentleness had a calming effect on me, and his knowledge of the Bible opened my eyes to its endless wisdom.

Clark was a symbol of everything I wanted to learn. Early on in our relationship he placed a Bible, anonymously, on my doorstep. The Bible became a permanent companion; and months afterwards, when Clark revealed himself as the secret donor, its value multiplied.

Our time together multiplied too, when he moved in with Ceil and me during his temporary unemployment. The live-in arrangement was my idea. I wanted Clark to share with us everything he knew about the word of God. Our relationship was a series of emotionally stirring, stimulating discussions. But I resisted when Clark suggested we tackle flying.

'There's nothing to be afraid of,' he promised.

'I can't.'

Clark grinned. 'What kind of a word is "can't", if you have God on your side?'

'All right,' I said. 'I can't. . . now. But soon.'

Flying seemed too great a hurdle, although my phobic attacks had decreased. I was still uneasy away from home, still wary in restaurants, still apprehensive when driving. But I managed. I was defeating the fear, slowly.

The greatest enemy to overcome, I realised now, was my physical craving for pills. I didn't subject my body to massive shock by undergoing cold turkey. But even gradual withdrawal forced up the anxiety level. My breathing would become laboured at unexpected moments, and I had to cope with nervous tics and spasms, tightness around the neck and the shakes.

Then I would feel, with euphoria, that I had done it; that the craving was conquered. This would go on for days, even weeks, until my need—triggered by some minor tension—would attack without warning.

I held onto my Bible; it bore the imprint of stressful fingers. I took it to business meetings and carried it to the post office. The book and I became Siamese twins.

The lure of the medicine cabinet remained strong, however. I resisted the urge to swallow away my panic and discomfort. Resisted until the compulsion grew too great, and I calmed myself with whatever sedative my fingers found first.

I beat off the symptoms with prayer, feeling the presence of an ally fighting along with me, encouraging me. A coach whispering in my ear, 'You want to stay in the game, don't you? Don't throw it all away now.'

It finally happened. The burning sensations, the involuntary leaping of muscles, the lump in the throat—they all retreated. Not in one magic instant, but steadily, slouching into corners to protect themselves against my growing faith.

Best of all, my wardrobe nightmares, the dreaded nocturnal reliving of child abuse, began to subside.

I continued to enjoy Bible studies and was sorry when Gabriel announced he was discontinuing them. He planned to travel with Debby after their marriage.

'Would anyone like to take the study over?' Gabriel asked, and I shot to my feet, volunteering my house, eager to carry on the weekly tradition.

Before long my Bible study welcomed many new people: Little Anthony and the Imperials, Nell Carter, Marilyn McCoo and Billy Davis, Charlene Tilton, manager Susan Munao, and producer Peter Engel.

I also formed close friendships with two other believers who attended, Bob Dylan and Donna Summer. My reunion with Bob took place at the Vineyard Church in the San Fernando Valley, fifteen years after our Columbia days. We had even more in common now; more than our Jewish upbringing and our songwriting careers.

Bob began to attend the study every week. He also went to classes at Bible college. These involvements took a great deal of time, yet he still found room to write his 'Slow Train Comin'' album.

Donna was equally dedicated. A former victim of depression—brought on by pressure, late hours and the travel that stardom demanded—she had found stability and inner peace through Jesus.

I admired the depth and passion of her feeling. Like Bob, she did more than pray; she set her views before the world, before every kind of audience. She risked disagreement from the press and from fans, but her courage never wavered.

I decided, from the start, that people who attended the Bible study would have privacy. I admired the privacy Alcoholics Anonymous offered its members and discouraged anyone from bringing tapes and scripts for celebrities who participated. Our study wasn't a conventional Hollywood party with Christian overtones. People like Donna Summer and Bob Dylan were entitled to worship, communicate with God, untroubled by business tensions they encountered during the day. Film, record and theatre people who came to pray could relax among others who understood their very special problems in the world.

I never stopped learning from these studies. I never lost my amazement that the wisdom of the Bible was so modern, so relevant, so psychologically sound.

Ceil couldn't believe the change in me.

'If this is what God does,' she said affectionately, 'how can I argue with it?' The words were light, but she felt my new serenity, my optimism and belief in myself and in our future.

Problems didn't disappear. Ceil and I were happily reunited and on a healthier footing than ever before, but there were times when she became depressed, times when I became angry, and times when we both felt let down by the other. The only difference was that we had common goals and a common faith that was enormously meaningful. We solved problems by pulling together, not apart.

Certain realities continued to exist. Despite everything, despite my newfound happiness, Larry refused to consider my conversion as anything but a temporary abberation.

My mother moved to California after the funeral. We found her a beautiful flat and she hated it, always saying, 'Why can't I live with you or Larry?' She found fault with the next place we suggested: 'Too small. The street is too noisy.'

She viewed the new brotherly closeness between Larry and me with discomfort and tried to set us against each other.

My instinctive reactions weren't totally changed; the change was in how I handled them. When my mother said, 'You're lucky Larry let you write the songs for *Seven Brides*,' my first response was to snap back, 'He commissioned me because I'm a good writer; luck had nothing to do with it.' Then I saw she wanted to provoke me, so I merely replied, 'Yes, I'm grateful to him.'

It's hard to surrender lifelong games, and the temptation always returns to fall into old patterns again. My faith provided the strength to resist self-destructive impulses.

'I hope both my sons win Tonys,' she said. Larry had

already won his Tony for *Applause.*

That left only me.

I prayed for relief from physical tension; physical tension that kept my stomach in perpetual knots.

One morning, while driving past the Beverly Hills school playground, I noticed a solitary runner. It was 6.30 in the morning.

I parked and went through the open fence to watch him. He turned and smiled. 'Come on.'

I shook my head and watched him gracefully complete another quarter of a mile.

'Let's walk,' the man said. He was in his mid-fifties, tall and trim, with sparse white hair.

We fell in step.

'How come you're out so early?' I asked.

'Like to get on the track before the crowd,' he said. We shook hands. 'I'm Jack McKee.'

'Al Kasha.' I didn't explain why I was out so early. I couldn't tell a complete stranger that it was therapy— retraining myself to drive by choosing a time when noise was at a minimum and roads were empty.

'I'd like to get in shape,' I told him.

'This is the way to do it.'

*OK, Lord*, I mumbled to myself. *If that's your plan, I'll be here tomorrow morning at 6.30.*

And I was. My brain was a lot more eager to participate than my body. I became unpleasantly familiar with every neglected muscle. All of them screamed in unison, 'Give me a break!'

My addiction started then—and I use that word deliberately. Addictive personalities will always be consumingly involved with *something*. The trick is to substitute constructive goals for the damaging ones. In place of uppers, I chose health foods. In place of Valium, I chose the relaxation of running.

At first I hauled my rusty, flabby machine around the

track, gasping for breath. And being so competitive, determined and dedicated, I pushed too hard, ran too far and
nearly ended up in hospital after the first week. Jack
begged me to take it slowly. But 'slowly' isn't a word
workaholics understand.

It took a while to achieve what runners call 'the
pain–pleasure phenomenon'. At the start it was all pain
and no pleasure. When runners turned up, I automatically
tried to match or surpass them. I saw myself entering
marathons before I could comfortably complete two miles.

Gradually, though, my trainers hooked onto those
'wings of joy' runners talk about. I increased my goal from
two miles to three, and I could feel my tension shedding
like dead skin. My mind was clear—clear the way it had
been under Ritalin, but bright and active without narcotics
to jolt it.

From then on, I never missed a morning if I could help
it. Ceil had to argue sense into me when I set off for the
track with a cold or flu. I felt closest to God on that track.
We had the majority of our conversations while I raced
along.

It was time to take on my next challenge—flying. I
walked into Clark's room one Saturday morning and said
simply, 'I'm ready.'

It wasn't Lindbergh and the Spirit of St Louis, but I had
the Spirit of God to get me to Los Angeles International
Airport.

'Hope we don't crash,' I said lightly.

Clark smiled and quoted a C.S. Lewis line: 'Don't worry
about death. . . you never know when it's coming.' He
added: 'Listen, I have news for you. If we crash I die too.
And I'm not interested in dying.'

I laughed. His logic was irrefutable, but I had to close
my eyes and think of God's words.

*Guard your heart and guard your mind. Think of beautiful
things.*

*Trust in God.*
*I can't control every situation.*
*Handle things moment by moment.*
*Manage rather than control.*
*Let go.*

The Western Airlines 707 took off for San Diego. My palms began to sweat.

'Easy,' whispered Clark.

The jet shivered in a sharp wind.

'Trust in God,' Clark reminded me.

The flight took twenty-five minutes. I can't say I had no phobic reactions at all. Nor did I stop praying until we were back on the ground. My fist almost snapped the little red Bible in half.

Flying was easier from then on, however. I went to San Diego with Clark the following weekend, and after that, to San Francisco. The distances grew longer, the destinations further away. Each flight felt more natural, less dangerous. I watched with admiration when I saw Clark doze off or become immersed in a flight magazine. He never paid attention when the stewardess delivered her obligatory safety demonstration before take-off.

Then came the day when I woke up actually looking forward to boarding a plane. Flying changed from therapy to adventure, joy and freedom.

I was no longer emotionally or physically grounded.

Larry continued to refuse to admit there were any changes in me. His only response to my Christianity was to ask, 'Is this a crutch?'

I told him I was happier than I'd ever been, and he said, 'It won't last. You'll come to your senses.'

It was a testament to my new faith that I stayed calm.

'Besides,' he added, 'these people are all judgemental. Look at your friend Donna Summer. She hates gays.'

'The whole point of Jesus is *not* to judge,' I protested. I told him that Donna Summer had been painted unfairly in the press; that in fact she loved all people and had a warm, generous heart.

He refused to believe it, and when I suggested that they meet, he quickly dismissed the idea.

Others shared Larry's viewpoint. At first it seemed as though I had committed professional suicide by embracing Christianity.

Even within the most innocuous and amiable of conversations, producers came up with such lines as, 'I don't like it when someone preaches at me.' 'If there's anything I can't stand, it's proselytising.' 'I'm entitled to be what I please.'

These arguments surfaced without any provocation. I was on my own spiritual search, not on a heavy-handed mission to push people towards my point of view. I did believe, deeply, that being a Christian brought love and peace, but I also knew that no one responded to being pushed or preached at. They only responded by observing something and quietly making up their own minds.

I know I lost jobs that first year. Producers baited me, slyly asking, 'Are you enjoying it?' Later on they'd sigh, 'I guess it works for him.' The implication was always: You're too *square* for Hollywood.

When people said, 'You're Jewish,' and I countered it with, 'Jesus was Jewish,' they frowned and dropped the subject. When I quoted Derek Prince, a great theological Oxford scholar, as saying, 'Christianity is a logical continuation of Judaism,' they stared at me in a patronising, pitying manner.

As a people pleaser, these negative reactions sorely tested me. I still had a need to be liked, but something infinitely bigger was operating now—a precious new existence, a life-enhancing value and belief system that had gathered up the troubled fragments of my personality and brought them together. Nothing was going to jeopardise that.

This was probably the happiest period of my life. There's a simplicity about identifying and meeting challenges. Like bowling pins, I selected them and knocked them down one by one.

When producers Mike Merrick and Don Gregory called me in 1979, though, I was afraid it would take more than a bowling pin or Bible to knock down the hurdle they presented.

'Hi, babe,' Mike's cheery, forceful voice boomed over the phone. 'Don and I talked it over and we're ready to move with *Copperfield*. We'd like to produce it on Broadway, open in early 1980. What do you say?'

*Maybe this is the supreme test*, I thought.

We gave the rights to Don and Mike. Their enthusiasm was contagious. They were also running a hot hand, with two hit touring companies of *Camelot* and *My Fair Lady*.

The show was shaping up well in its St Louis trial run, and I allowed myself a few days of cautious optimism. Then Mike Merrick approached us unexpectedly and said he and Don needed $150,000. One of their backers, a Greek tycoon, had dropped out.

'Happened last week,' said Mike. 'Don and I didn't want to worry you guys, but now we need the money.'

'And if we can't find it?' Joel asked.

'Well, we can open,' said Mike. 'But there's nothing in the kitty to keep us going. Either we get raves or we close. We can't put up a fight.'

Back in California, running had helped me to get rid of tension. I turned to it again when we arrived in Manhattan, racing along the cold streets, as though the answers I needed were contained in the gusty March wind. If no other time was available I ran at night, ignoring Ceil's warnings that Manhattan was fraught with danger.

Joel and Jill were playing out the last destructive chapter of their control struggle. She was still pushing him to eat;

he still resisted, then complied. As a result Joel was seriously overweight and Jill down to just over 6st. They were exhausted by the game, yet incapable of stopping it; addicted to patterns that were destroying them. I wondered if Joel would bail out in time to save himself.

We continued with *Copperfield* rewrites, doing many of them at our old haunt the Pink Cloud. It had brought good fortune before; maybe it would again. The omelettes were just as underdone and tasteless, the juice just as watery. But there was comfort in a greasy spoon that represented youthful hope and optimism.

Our cast gave it their all, and it was a superbly talented group: Mary Elizabeth Mastrantonio, who became a big star in such films as *Robin Hood* and *The Colour of Money*; Brian Matthews, portraying David with charisma and flair; and a very young Christian Slater.

The conflict between Joel and Jill worsened. I wasn't in good shape either. My mother, back in Los Angeles, had fainted on the street. A visit to her doctor disclosed inoperable cancer.

I felt guilty that I wasn't with her. Larry wasn't at her bedside either. He was touring with his own musical production *Woman of the Year*, starring Lauren Bacall. At dinner, Larry informed me that he was opening his show two days before *Copperfield*.

'I pray you both get Tonys,' my mother said, attempting to stir up old animosities. Tired as she was, her focus remained relentless.

Though Joel and I were rewriting until opening night, I jumped on a plane to see her. I flew back that same evening. A few days later I returned to the hospital. After a while I couldn't tell the difference between air and solid ground. The juxtaposition of writing and watching my mother slowly die turned the last weeks before the show into an unending nightmare.

My mother repeatedly asked, 'Is Larry all right? He isn't

working too hard, is he?'

'He's fine.'

'I worry so much about him. You don't know the blood the theatre takes from Larry.'

'Yes I do. Believe me, Mum, I do.'

*Woman of the Year* opened on a Sunday, and *Copperfield* on a Tuesday. The reviews for *Woman* were generally good. Frank Rich of the *Times* published his all-important notice and determined the play's outcome. He felt, on the basis of Lauren Bacall's star quality, that the show worked.

'Always come to Broadway with a star,' Larry had told me. We had arrived with unknowns—great talents and *future* stars, but still unfamiliar to the theatre-going public.

*Copperfield* was, and continued to be, an audience pleaser in previews. Jose Ferrer and Otto Preminger were among the celebrities who attended the opening night and their lavish praise gave us hope.

Clive Barnes of the *New York Post* raved. The *New York Times* liked our score, said it was tuneful, but objected to certain liberties we had taken with Dickens.

*Woman of the Year* became a hit for Larry; *Copperfield*'s run turned out to be less than we had hoped for.

## 15

# *Only With Love Can We Climb*

But God, I was learning, often has a surprise up his sleeve, and when Tony nominations were announced, Larry and I were both among the nominees: he as producer; Joel and I for our *Copperfield* score.

'See,' I told Joel. 'There *was* a reason. This is God's way of telling us to try again.'

He was also saying, I felt, that positive, upbeat shows could survive and triumph. In one form or another, they would gain recognition. I was grateful to the Tony committee for reinforcing that belief.

I was sensible enough to recognise that we had little chance of winning. The gifted Kander and Ebb, who had written *Chicago* and *Cabaret*, were front-runners for *Woman of the Year*.

Three weeks prior to the award ceremonies, my mother's condition took a sharp turn for the worse. Larry and I were planning to meet at the hospital. Ceil and I arrived first.

My mother looked terrible. Her shrunken, sallow face brought back images of my father in his last days. She was smiling, however.

'Alfred, do you know who just called me? Dom DeLuise. He said he was a friend of yours, and he wanted me to get well soon.'

A gesture like that was typical of Dom. Dom wasn't just a superb comic, he was a solicitous human being—unquestionably the sweetest man in Hollywood.

'He said he might come over and see me.'

'If he said so, he will.'

'I'm so proud of you, Alfred.'

'Thank you, Ma.'

'I know you and Larry will both win.'

'You'll know when we do, if you keep your TV on.'

'Lean over, darling.'

I did, and she kissed me.

'You know,' she said, 'if you had only let Larry direct *Copperfield*, you would have won a Tony for sure.'

'Ma, don't try to talk.'

'He would have done it so much better.'

*How do you know? You never even saw it!*

'Lawrence is so talented.' Then, 'I have two wonderful boys. God bless you both.'

She settled back on her pillow. 'I'll pray you win. If I could, I'd go to the temple. Maybe I still can. . . go to the temple.'

'Thank you, Ma.'

Her mood changed. A streak of alarm crossed her pale face.

'Alfred, I just remembered something. I have to get up.'

'You can't get up, Ma. You're tired. Relax.'

'I have to get to the bank.'

'The bank?'

Her mind was slipping away. She beckoned to the nurse.

'You've got to get me to the bank.' Her tone turned shrill, frantic. 'Please.'

'Tomorrow, Ma, tomorrow.'

She grabbed at my shirt. 'Do you promise?'

'I promise.'

'You're a good son, L'Alfred. And you too, Ceil darling. You've been a good daughter.'

My mother died during the night. Three days later her will was read, and the contents of her jealously guarded blue bag were distributed. She left two-thirds to my brother, one-third to me.

Nothing to Dana.

'It's got to be a mistake,' said Ceil, speaking the words I was incapable of forming.

Larry put his hand on my shoulder. He was as totally unprepared as I was.

*You've got to get me to the bank.*

Was that the reason for my mother's last-minute agitation? A change of heart? Had she felt guilty in those final hours—guilty about slighting one son in favour of another? Guilty of overlooking her beautiful granddaughter; the granddaughter who had always been considerate and affectionate to her; who had listened to her grievances with love and sympathy?

I would never know.

On 10th June 1980, the Tony Committee announced its winners on TV. Ceil squeezed my hand until my knuckles burned. Joel sat with his sister Madeleine. His domestic situation was deteriorating, and Jill had chosen to remain in California.

*Woman of the Year* won for Best Score (among the four Tonys my brother collected). I reminded myself, *There's a reason.* I was too drained from my mother's death and from the trauma of the will to attach much importance to the award. Somehow I made it through the elaborate dinner afterwards.

'I promise you one thing,' Larry said, when we discussed *Seven Brides* and its proposed opening on Broadway the following year. 'I'm going to put Mother's money behind the show, to give it a healthy budget and pay for the best people.'

I was happy, but I couldn't help laughing at the irony. Because it was so against everything in her nature to take risks with money, to speculate. All her life, she had hoarded every penny, hidden all her assets from her husband and sons. One bed, cockroaches, broken furniture, deprivation on all levels—to gather up the backing for a Broadway musical.

Rose Kasha, the Broadway angel.

Rose Kasha, who would rather walk than take a bus; who bought all her clothes in the sales; who resisted giving birthday or Christmas presents to the end of her days—a posthumous Broadway investor.

The new touring company of *Seven Brides*, starring Debby Boone, proved to be as commercially successful as the old one with Jane and Howard. Debby was outstanding in the part: a capable actress, a superb singer, a nimble dancer. Her faith was an intrinsic part of her, and it added an extra dimension to her work. I never saw any let up in energy, honesty or vocal perfection.

A year later Joel and I were nominated for another Tony. We didn't win, but the show became a permanent touring item, in the United States and abroad. *Seven Brides* broke records at London's Old Vic, and became a staple in Australia, New Zealand, Italy and Spain. Its long life refuelled our drive to continue in the theatre and to work on projects we believed in.

In 1982, unfortunately, our eighteen-year partnership fell apart. Joel and Jill decided to give their marriage one last chance, unencumbered by pressure, and spent most of their time in their Arrowhead home.

The mountain calm and beauty of Arrowhead had come to symbolise, in Jill's mind, an escape from friction, from competing, from the world of show business. She had temporarily given up her own songwriting career to become a photo-journalist. She encouraged Joel to write a novel, saying, 'It's a quiet way of life, without all those producers and publishers breathing down your neck. You can work alone.' 'Alone' meant a simple life that included long walks, swimming, riding and a minimum of entertaining.

Her own intense nature found the uncluttered calm of

mountain living a relief. Joel, though, missed the buzzing activity of Los Angeles. Bronx-born, a film addict, he had difficulty with the fact that Lake Arrowhead lacked cinemas. Joel had nursed a desire to be a film critic and commentator all his life, which he later fulfilled with his best-selling book *Rating the Movie Stars*. 'Even so,' he insisted, 'I have to try; give it my best shot. Jill and I love each other.' He added, 'It's not that we can't write.'

'Of course we can write,' I agreed. 'You can drive to Hollywood, or I can come to the mountains.'

But I knew better. It took energy to make a faltering marriage work, and the geographical problems were a serious deterrent to regular creativity.

More crucially, I recognised that Joel's work would have to take a distinct second to his personal relationship. I know many relationships function that way. I've always felt, though—and still do—that a man's work is a basic part of him. I know how precious family and friends are, but I believe a man's work is a fundamental outgrowth of who he is.

In any case, I felt sad about the break. Sad for all the lost dreams, the plans Joel and I had made. The films, books and shows that were never to be; the Rodgers and Hammerstein heirs we would never become. Ceil regretted the split as much as I did.

Joel and I met occasionally for lunch, and we would muse vaguely about 'getting together to write'. Once or twice we did actually start a song, but we rarely finished it; and when we did, it wasn't up to our old standard.

'Next time we'll get it,' Joel would say, and both of us felt angry and depressed simultaneously. Gradually we stopped getting in touch, and I set about organising a separate life.

I taught songwriting at churches and universities. I also launched a lecture tour, speaking about the influence of Christianity on modern music. It was exhilarating to move freely and accept engagements without paralysing phobic symptoms.

During one of the tours I appeared on a small Philadelphia TV channel. The guest immediately before me was a young woman who described her years of agoraphobia. Even though my topic on the show was songwriting, I mentioned to the announcer that I had been a victim of the same phobia.

Instead of rushing past my remark, he made it the basis for the entire interview. He wanted to know why an Oscar winner, a man who had succeeded in a difficult, competitive profession, would fall prey to incapacitating phobic illness. I answered gladly, seizing the chance to share my story with a broad audience. The TV company was deluged with calls, and I was invited back the following week to give a more detailed account of my recovery.

In every interview after that, I referred to my struggle with phobic illness. I received encouragement from a remarkable pastor named Jess Moody. Jess was a tall, imposing man with a gloriously playful sense of humour and direct, engaging honesty. Although he grew up on a farm in Muleshoe, Texas, and I came from the streets of Brooklyn, we were of one mind and heart from our first meeting.

'You have an important story,' Jess said, 'and because you're a public figure, you can have a strong effect. You're already helping people. Just keep on being real. Don't make speeches. Remember, more people tell their stories to barmaids than pastors, so be a *friend*.'

That advice stayed with me when I appeared on other TV shows, both Christian and secular. I became more and more determined to reach phobic sufferers on a national level.

Oddly enough, publicity began to appear, discrediting me, implying that my Christianity was suspect because I worked actively in Hollywood. The more conservative elements of Christianity claimed that Hollywood presented a negative role model. Violence and sex were dominant, and millions of people were pouring into cinemas to see these films rather than the positive ones.

My conscience was clear on that score: Joel and I had devoted our lives to family entertainment, and we weren't the only ones. Children had the benefit of great entertainments such as *Beauty and the Beast* and *Aladdin*. And there were first-rate adult films that didn't depend for their impact on gratuitous violence or sex: *Howard's End*, *A River Runs Through It*, *Quiz Show*, *The Age of Innocence* and *Shadowlands*.

Nevertheless, many films contained controversial and deeply questionable material; films such as *Silence of the Lambs, Basic Instinct* and *Cape Fear*.

What these films did have, however, was uniform expertise in directing, acting and writing.

My response was to urge Christians not to support films that violated their values, but rather to back motion pictures that carried wholesome and positive messages. It wasn't enough to say, 'Why don't the studios do more pictures like *Chariots of Fire?*' They had to band together and create their own pictures.

Several Christian-backed motion pictures had failed with the general public, and the makers were indignant, but the answer was obvious. Most of them were poorly made.

It wasn't enough for a Christian, or religious-themed, film to be on the side of the angels. It had to put across its message through a well-integrated story and realistic characters. It couldn't just preach—the message had to grow organically out of the material. And it also had to be of the same professional quality that the unpalatable studio-produced films were! It had to be well-written, acted and directed. Only then could a Christian picture compete with needlessly violent 18-rated products.

Years later, Joel and I were fortunate enough to write the music for a project that demonstrated my point. The film, financed by the Trinity Broadcasting Network, was entitled *China Cry*. Michael Medved, a courageous and perceptive critic, stated in his bestseller, *Hollywood Vs. America*:

> Its emotional impact is undeniable. Both times I've watched it, audience members wept openly at its true story of a young mother who undergoes a religious conversion while suffering brutal persecution at the hands of the Chinese communists . . . the biggest surprise of this offbeat production is its remarkable performance at the box office. It easily clobbered such films as *Goodfellas, Rocky V* or *Predator II*.

*China Cry* was superbly crafted on every level. It included a magnificent lead performance by Julia Nickson-Soul, and people flocked to see it in record numbers. Such success brought back Oscar Hammerstein's line to me when I was a child, 'People will always remember hope.'

I'm a great believer in edifying subject matter—as my career has proved—but we have to train and encourage talented young film-makers to convey that message with expertise, in a way the general public will respond to.

Despite the voices raised against me for my long-term Hollywood background, I was able to reach the public. When I appeared on television, I assured viewers that there was nothing to be ashamed of in having agoraphobia, and begged them to join any reputable group specialising in phobic treatment. I knew from experience that sharing with other people would eliminate feelings of isolation and hopelessness.

I continued to address many of my comments directly to the male agoraphobic. I knew, more than ever, that admitting this weakness clashed with a man's efforts to be strong and to convey a macho image. Powerful executives and businessmen hated to say they were beaten up by their fathers; hated to admit their lifelong fear of authoritative male peers. I reassured them that their fear, which I had always shared, was nothing to be ashamed of; that these terrors, developed in childhood, no longer had any validity.

Within weeks letters poured in from agoraphobics around the country—men and women. All of them had been through pressures I had described. Many were desperate.

'I don't feel self-respect any more. . .'

'I'm too ashamed even to make love to my wife. . .'

'How could I be so *weak*? I want to be strong for her. I want her to feel she can lean on me.'

'I'm afraid to tell my wife. . . she'll worry that I can't support her. . .'

'I'm afraid to tell my kids. They won't look up to me any more.'

'I'm afraid to tell my boss. He'll sack me.'

Some men told me they had taken jobs which were beneath them both financially and creatively in order to be close to home. One film editor described his terror when he was asked to go out of the office at lunchtime to bring back sandwiches for his co-workers. He had hidden in the toilets, gathering up courage, feeling like a condemned man with every step towards a bakery that was only across the street.

I answered all the letters, reminding each person to stand firm when symptoms recurred; stand firm and trust in God's help. 'Remember,' I wrote, 'every minute you stand firm is more ammunition against panic.'

It came to me, while writing to a phobic housewife who had spent the past five years indoors, that mail or even TV was too impersonal for totally meaningful contact. TERRAP proved beneficial to agoraphobics who could, with great difficulty, force themselves to leave home for short periods of time. But what of victims who *never* ventured from home base? They had to see an individual up close, with the same affliction they had; see that he had beaten it, stepped out into the sunlight, made it through traffic, moved easily in crowded shopping centres.

I brought my own special phobic cure door to door. I became a salesman for serenity and freedom.

'No, I can't go out there,' was the statement that greeted me over and over again.

'I did it. So can you. Just take one step at a time. We'll try standing in the street and taking a short walk. Next week we'll walk a little further. And I'll be with you.'

I repeatedly emphasised that they didn't have to cover miles immediately, or drive to the other end of town. Half a block was a start. Sitting in a car was progress. Or parking near a supermarket without going inside.

Eventually, since I was in show business, I received calls from well-known people who were either agoraphobics themselves or had agoraphobics in their families. A world-famous director, for whom Joel and I had written a score, contacted me. His wife had not left their Beverly Hills home for three years.

'You weren't really an agoraphobic,' she told me. Her blue eyes had a permanent squint, even in the safety of her living room, as though hiding from any brightness outside. 'Or else you'd be. . . '

'Nervous? Afraid? That's what I'm trying to show you. I *was* all those things. I got over it. So can you.'

She trembled. Just then we heard a dustcart squealing to a stop. It made a deafening noise.

'It's only a lorry,' I said.

Her thoughts rang out as clearly as if they were blasting through a stereo speaker: *It's dangerous out there. Unknown horrors are waiting. I'll lose all control; humiliate myself; be a failure, a laughing-stock.*

Within the next three months, I persuaded her to walk

with me. Often she fled back, slamming her door. I would call and she'd refuse to talk to me, or if I came to the house, she'd plead to be excused from our little expeditions.

I couldn't get her to a phobic centre, but I spoke to her about God; about visualising his image as positive reinforcement. I quoted a biblical passage: 'Fear not, there is nothing to fear for I am with you.' We prayed together.

My own attitudes about phobic treatment were crystallising. The missing link, spirituality, had become obvious to me. Most of the courses and literature I had observed only zeroed in on psychological and medical aids, and these were fine—as far as they went. But the healing power of prayer was omitted.

I had discovered the force of that healing power, and I knew it would work wonders. Visualisation, meditation and proper nutrition were the foundation of treatment; prayer was the roof.

A year later the director's wife drove to San Diego, her first substantial trip behind the wheel. She still has momentary setbacks, but I know her progress will be continuous from now on.

I worked with a rock star whose image was synonymous with sexuality. Millions of women responded to his virility and animal appeal. Twenty-four, 6ft 2in, a dynamo on stage, Chet (a pseudonym) nearly fainted at the prospect of sitting in a crowded restaurant. I reassured him that although he felt like the forgotten agoraphobic, he wasn't. I hadn't forgotten him, and support groups and friends willing to help hadn't forgotten him either. Repeated attempts to confront his fear, along with visualisation and prayer, finally gave him the courage to overcome the block.

I saw renowned producers, athletes, fashion designers and heads of corporations break out in a cold, trembling sweat when they had to take a lift. I could no longer doubt that phobic illness was a national epidemic. It was an epidemic that required armies of new recruits from every quarter.

I spoke to the families of agoraphobics and stressed the importance of their constructive participation. It wasn't enough to tolerate phobic behaviour and cover up for it. Nor could a phobic be pushed and criticised into a cure, as certain husbands and wives of phobic victims mistakenly tried to do. Relatives had to learn to work with those in the grip of agoraphobia. They had to become, in effect, live-in phobia therapists. They had to be taught techniques most beneficial to their phobically imprisoned loved ones.

I supplied specific information for them through an organisation I started, Faith Over Fear (FOF), which laid out known therapeutic methods along with the sayings and scriptures that had helped me towards recovery.

The ranks of door-to-door phobic therapists grew. I called for volunteers through every media channel available.

The words of Pastor Jack Hayford rang in my ears: 'When a miracle happens to you, you must tell people about it and pass it on.' Excitement filled me when I saw the stirring of hope on previously despairing faces. Sometimes I looked at their windows when leaving them. I caught them staring at me, waving, watching. I felt their burning gazes as I crossed the street and got into my car. I waved back and made gestures of victory.

I was gratified to learn that the insights God had given me were making an impact. One Arizona woman, who had been housebound for eighteen years, drove twenty-two blocks with her grandchild. Today she moves about freely, with total confidence. A forty-year-old man from Oregon called and said he had seen me on TV and had found the courage to walk ten blocks—seven more than he had ever gone. Now he travels with no fear.

When I read in *Variety* that *Seven Brides* was nominated for a Best Score Tony, I called Lake Arrowhead to share the exciting news with Joel. Jill answered and told me Joel was living in LA. She didn't pursue the subject and I didn't either; but when I tracked Joel down, he admitted that he and Jill were separated and expected to get a divorce.

Over lunch at the Old World Restaurant in Beverly Hills, he furnished more details.

'They tell you that all you have to do is love each other and it'll work out all right. I guess that's why we kept hanging on. Because we *did* love each other. We still do. And yet we couldn't agree on how to live.' He laughed. 'Anyway, I've got a big city mentality. I'm not a mountain climber or a hunter. I'd rather die on a film set with sheet music in my hand than on the ski slopes. I knew it was time to get back to civilisation when I found three coyotes sitting in my garden.'

He turned thoughtful. 'It all seemed to get out of hand. Funnily enough, Jill's working in therapy now, at a hospital, helping alcoholics. She's even planning to go back to school in order to get her qualifications.'

I watched him trying to handle the situation with objectivity and understanding. Then, inevitably, he exploded with a normal, spontaneous outburst.

'I *hate* all this. It's murder. You put so much into something. . .'

'I know.'

'What do you do with all that emotion? Emotion you've built up over fifteen years? All the anger, all the pain.'

'You pour it back into the Pink Cloud.'

For the first time that afternoon, Joel laughed.

'I'm serious. Think how it all began, and how much hope we had for the future. All the things we wanted to do.'

'You're right,' he said. 'You can't keep two guys from Brooklyn and the Bronx down.'

All the obstacles—real and imagined—were clearing, leaving the road free to do what we loved above anything else.

To write.

'I still want us to be Rodgers and Hammerstein,' I said.

'Great.'

'No!' My throat went dry. 'Let's change that. Let's *not* be Rodgers and Hammerstein.'

I thought of all the press releases I had seen through the years: Another Streisand. Another Sinatra. Another Dylan.

I was suddenly swept up in an emotion I had never expected to feel: the intense, overpowering desire to be myself.

'Let's be Kasha and Hirschhorn,' I announced.

We toasted with two glasses of orange juice.

'We can stand for what they stood for, but let's be Kasha and Hirschhorn, and be the best at that—the *very* best— that we can possibly be.'

It was cloudy on the drive down to Hillside Memorial, but I noticed the sun breaking through by the time I passed the gate.

> ROSE KASHA
> MOTHER OF LAWRENCE AND ALFRED
> WIFE OF IRVING
> 1910–1980

'Hello, Ma,' I said into the still air. 'I'm sorry I haven't been here for a while.'

I took a deep breath.

'You know, Ma, I believe in God now. . . like I never did before. It's such a relief when you have faith. I wish you could have known what it was like.'

The sun grew hotter; I felt sweat on my forehead.

'I don't want to be angry any more,' I told her. 'I don't

want to hold on to things—like the will, and all those times when I brought victory home and you kept saying, "Not enough, not enough." What more could I have done?'

And the answer came to me: nothing. Because constant dissatisfaction was my mother's way of holding on to me and to Larry. If she withheld her approval, we would always be tied to her by a compulsive desire to please.

'You could have trusted my love,' I said, with belated understanding. 'You could have said I did a good job, and I'd still have been there.'

I hadn't expected to cry. The tears surprised me. I hadn't cried when she was dying, the way Larry had.

For a minute I surrendered to the tears; to my last, infantile yearning for a replay, a chance to start again and get it right.

'Shave me, Alfred. Shave me, son,' I heard my father say. At least that moment had put a seal on our relationship—given it some kind of conclusion. I could come to terms with my father's violence, grasp the frustrations that had turned him into a child abuser. But the relationship between my mother and me had been left open-ended.

And that other question, always nagging at me, sprang out again, more insistently than ever: 'Why didn't you ever leave my father? Why didn't you let me help you, support you? Rescue you?'

'Save me, Alfred,' I heard my mother say.

It was time to face the unfaceable; to answer my own question with a truth I could never bear to acknowledge.

*She loved him.*

If she had been serious about divorce, about the way out, she would have done it. 'If I leave, what will happen to the business?' she had asked me. But of course, if they had broken up and she had managed the business alone, it would have gone on, even improved, without my father's drinking and hell-raising.

She would have let the policemen take him away when he beat us.

She would have found her own flat as soon as Larry and I had the means to support her.

Understanding brought an emotion I had never been able to feel for my mother before: pity. Because she had suffered. The suffering had been self-inflicted, the scars her own doing. But that didn't make them any less real.

'I forgive you, Ma,' I said to the sun-washed stone, 'if you'll forgive me. I know you hear me. Let's start again. It's never too late.'

I knelt, touched the stone and left.

During the next seven years, I kept hoping for a genuine and complete reconciliation with Larry. My mother and father were no longer around to stir up our childhood rivalry. We were older, more established in our professions. Larry never criticised my spiritual pursuits; I never criticised his lifestyle. We spent Thanksgiving and Christmas together as a family, talking pleasantly and impersonally about our work.

It was different with my daughter. She opened up completely to Larry, and he became her second father, fan and best friend. If I had told him my house was on fire, he'd have registered a mild reaction, yet when Dana wanted to show him a new pair of shoes, he reacted as if an epic event had taken place. She talked about her teachers, her classmates, her boyfriends, new hairstyle, her homework. Whatever it was, he offered his complete and undivided attention.

I couldn't help feeling a little envious. She was my daughter, and I wanted her to have a warm relationship with her uncle. But I did wish he had given a tenth of that commitment to me.

Their closeness reached its height as Dana entered adolescence. Now she was his girlfriend, his pal, his confidante. She was invited to his parties; Ceil and I weren't.

Dana was with Larry when he and Darryl quarrelled

and ended their relationship. She held his hand through the agonising months that followed. It was Dana who stayed on the phone with him, hour after hour, when he was unable to concentrate on work, unable to eat, unable to do anything but focus on the despair of losing Darryl.

'Darryl started seeing someone else,' Dana explained, 'but he saw straight away that it was a mistake. He'd do anything to get back with Uncle Larry. They still love each other, but one of them has to make the first move.'

I refused to take it as seriously as Dana did. In the gay life, love affairs were fleeting. If you lost one lover, another quickly came along to replace him. Dana thought my response was insensitive. I know now that she was right.

Because of my attitude, Larry couldn't confide in me. He pretended everything was fine, that losing Darryl didn't matter, when I knew from Dana that he had been on the verge of suicide.

My daughter spent more time in his house than in her own, meeting superstars like Lauren Bacall, Alexis Smith, Debbie Reynolds, John Raitt, Hal Linden and Raquel Welch. Dana had a natural, self-effacing charm, and this exposure to theatrical celebrities helped her to gain sophistication and a sense of complete comfort in the company of all kinds of people. Through Larry, she developed into a delightfully confident, skilful hostess.

When Larry became the co-executive producer of CBS' long-running series *Knots Landing*, Dana attended every filming. As usual, they shared all the ups and downs of the soap opera, every behind-the-scenes intrigue, every temperamental outburst from the stars. People always wanted to know what was going to happen a week later, and Dana was the only one who got the inside information. Larry swore her to secrecy and she kept her vow.

I only heard the stories second hand, so it came as a tremendous surprise when Larry asked Joel and me to score several of the show's episodes.

The scoring process was enjoyable, since soap operas offer arrangers an opportunity to write in a variety of moods. When a heroine wasn't being kidnapped, she was tampering with a car and sending a rival to her doom. Or a hero (who wanted too much money) was written out of the series, and had to die lingeringly in a hospital to the accompaniment of lush, melodramatic strings. Larry's behaviour about our participation was also uncharacteristic. Ordinarily the most hands-on of all producers, he simply said, 'Do what you think is right. I trust you.' Joel and I were flattered but puzzled, even though the actors and other producers were completely satisfied with our work.

It was the first time in our lives that I had ever seen my brother so quiet—or so reflective. When I tried to probe, he claimed he was wrestling with a persistent stomach bug.

Dana was concerned too, and urged him to see a doctor. By now he was losing weight. His brisk, efficient stride had become a slow, unsteady shuffle.

'This stomach bug is worse,' he complained. 'It must be some kind of strange virus.'

I called Larry's doctor, Harlan Kravitz, and Doctor Kravitz confirmed the virus theory. Ceil, Dana and I weren't convinced.

A final clue to the seriousness of his condition was revealed when Larry stayed away from work for three days in a row. My brother was conscientious to a fault; a fanatic worker who shouldered his own responsibilities and everyone else's as well. He also had a fear—completely unfounded, since he was superb at his job—that the network would sack him for the most trivial mistake.

My questions provoked him to anger, and he kept repeating, 'I'm fine, I'm fine. Don't flutter over me like a mother hen.'

The pretence was abandoned at last when he called me at six in the morning and begged me to come over. He wanted me to take him to the doctor for tests.

I hadn't seen my brother for a week, and the change was shocking. His clothes hung on him. He had heavy black circles around his eyes. And he could hardly raise his voice above a whisper.

Another sign alarmed me: the fact that he permitted me to drive. Larry never let anyone drive; he had a greater need for control than any human being I've ever known.

Doctor Kravitz persisted in saying that the problem was flu or a virus. But he did add, offhandedly, that if matters didn't improve in a day or two, he might consider sending my brother to hospital.

I know Larry wasn't thinking rationally when he asked me to go to the pharmacy downstairs and pick up his prescription. The drug was leucovorin. I'd seen that name in an article about AIDS patients.

Too staggered to be casual and diplomatic, I blurted out on the way home, 'Larry, you don't have AIDS, do you?'

The dreaded word roused him from his weak, lethargic state. His eyes blazed and he looked as if he wanted to hit me.

'Don't. . . ever. . . say that to me again!' he said. 'Not ever!'

Shortly afterwards the energy born of anger deserted him and he fell asleep, his head on my shoulder.

# 16

# *Hospital—1990*

No matter what food the nurses brought, Larry only wanted ice cream.

His desire went beyond the fact that ice cream was easy to swallow, and all other foods had become an excruciating chore. He was reaching back to a more hopeful period of our lives, when he would eat one full tub after another.

These ice cream binges occurred long before he discovered weight lifting; long before he put such disciplines on his body. Long before stressful opening nights and failed relationships and a year-long bout of hepatitis. The way he stared at the ice cream placed before him, I got the feeling he perceived it as rescue, as a cure-all more powerful than any of the injections and medicines the doctors were giving him.

The other thing that soothed my brother, and somehow eradicated his fear, was the presence of Dana. Dana and he had developed a shorthand, loving, unspoken communication between them.

Dana had a gentle, caring quality. She was everything to Larry—friend, pupil, admirer, daughter. To her, Uncle Larry was a combination of P.T. Barnum and Peter Pan. He had exposed her to great theatre, wonderful music; he had taken her on the road when his production of *Singing in the Rain* was in Dallas; when *Seven Brides* opened in St Louis. And he had been there, steadfastly, during Dana's long recuperation from pneumonia in 1989.

Now it was Larry who was unwell and I could see her trying to be brave. Ceil kept busy, plumping pillows, putting magazines in their proper places—anything to distract herself from the fragile, withered brother-in-law who had once been so powerful and intimidating.

When Larry had had enough ice cream, Dana fed him chicken soup. She was the only one he allowed in the room when he needed to be fed.

'Where's Kelly?'

Ceil, Dana and I looked at each other, not knowing what to answer. Kelly had been Larry's last lover, and he had died of AIDS just two months before.

'He'll be calling in later,' I said, afraid to upset him.

'Kelly . . .' He could hardly summon the strength to pronounce the name.

None of us had asked the question, knowing we never could: was Kelly responsible for giving my brother AIDS?

And in the end, it didn't matter. The knowledge couldn't save Larry.

His speech was beginning to slur, and when he tried to write, the letters zig-zagged crookedly up and down the page. This puzzled me, because I had seen AIDS patients before and none of them—no matter how weak, no matter how terminal—had exhibited Larry's personality or motor control symptoms.

'Larry has a syphilitic virus,' explained one of the doctors. 'It affects the brain. Every patient is affected differently.'

The worst thing of all was Larry's anxious pleas to be taken home.

'I'll be all right . . . if you just take me home,' Larry kept repeating. I was beginning to believe that too, clutching at straws, wanting to believe anything that would make a miraculous, last-minute rescue possible.

Even during the night, I would be awakened by Larry's voice, begging, 'Al. . . talk to the hospital. I want to go home.'

I distracted him from this obsession by reading passages from his favourite novels and plays, as well as psalms and the parables of Jesus.

But the time came when Larry no longer asked me if he could go home, and I stopped letting him think it was a possibility. Instead, he wanted to know, 'Why do they have to do so many tests?' as a parade of doctors poured in periodically to examine him.

I felt the same way. It was a refined form of torture, checking his heart, his kidneys, every part of his anatomy. The medical bills rose astronomically, and deep down I knew all these examinations were unnecessary, particularly after Doctor Kravitz told me that Larry had—at the very most—six to eight weeks.

By now, Larry's colleagues and friends were growing anxious. Only a few were allowed to visit, and Larry made me promise to hide the facts of his condition.

I pleaded with the doctors not to put him on the same floor with other AIDS patients. He didn't want the press to know, fearing it would harm the ratings of *Knots Landing*, and he worried it would have a detrimental effect on his health insurance payments. The doctors refused, but my tenacity finally won them over.

'Say it's cancer,' Larry begged me. 'Say it's a brain tumor. But don't let anyone know. Especially Darryl.'

'He's been calling every hour from New York.'

'No. I want him to remember me the way I was.'

'He doesn't care,' I insisted. 'He wants to be with you.'

'Seeing him now would hurt too much.'

My brother maintained his composure right to the end. The only time I saw him cry was when he mentioned Darryl. I had never really allowed myself to face—or under-stand—the depth of the love Larry and Darryl shared. But they had, in reality, spent fifteen years together—socialising, writing, producing, creating a shared existence.

I did my best to be convincing, but no one totally believed my story. Larry's gay friends were particularly sceptical. All of them had experienced devastating losses; had seen their loved ones waste away from the ravages of AIDS. They instinctively suspected the truth.

It was obvious that the people in my brother's life blamed me. They felt shut out, and thought I was taking over in a high-handed way.

When I said, 'Larry can't see anyone now,' they demanded to speak to him themselves. I was uncharacteristically firm and relentlessly determined to shield my brother. In the past, my need to be liked, my need to 'be nice', would have caused tremendous inner conflict in the face of their demands. But love for Larry overrode that need.

Oddly enough, one of the few exceptions Larry made to his 'no-visitors' edict was Donna Summer. It was as if he needed to know, to *verify*, that she was truly in his corner; a friend and not someone who wanted to judge him.

I think it gave him great comfort when she kissed him and prayed for his recovery.

When he was strong enough to talk, we reviewed our history together. Larry no longer had the need to pretend. He saw that I accepted him totally, in a non-judgemental way.

He talked to Joel and me about the legendary female stars he had worked with—Barbra Streisand (whom he had directed in the London production of *Funny Girl* and who had given him his first cat, Sadie), Ginger Rogers (whom he had directed in the London production of *Mame*), Lucie Arnaz, Debbie Reynolds, Ava Gardner and Michele Lee—and how much the associations had meant to him.

'I wonder if I've done enough with my life,' Larry said. Joel and I both reminded him of his accomplishments, and how much joy they had brought to the world: *Applause, Woman of the Year, Seven Brides for Seven Brothers, She Loves*

*Me, Seesaw* and *Funny Girl*.

'But there's so much more to do,' he said. 'When I'm better, let's write a book about the theatre. . . about the actresses I've known—we can call it "Larry's Ladies" '.

'As soon as you get home,' I promised him, taking notes as he dictated one colourful anecdote after another.

'Are you taking care of Sam?' he asked.

Sam was Larry's dog: a big, lovable, energetic English Springer. Larry worried about Sam like the most nervous, over-protective mother.

'He's fine.'

'And is Flora coming every day? I want the house to be well taken care of.'

I had to laugh. In the midst of irreversible calamity, Larry still lived in panic that his house wouldn't be clean.

I told him that Ceil and Dana were there all the time, looking after Sam, walking him and keeping things in order.

Throughout this painful time, I took comfort from the teachings of two highly-regarded preachers—Jack Hayford and Derek Prince.

Jack Hayford was the most compassionate man I'd ever met. Tall, with a long angular face and a loving, sensitive personality, he often broke down during sermons while talking about God, feeling the Spirit of God work through him.

His American quality contrasted strikingly with Derek Prince's distinctively British speech and manner. Prince spoke passionately about Jesus, how he healed people.

These two men of towering vision and spiritual strength were role models for me. They were tremendously honest and sincere. Both explained the essence of faith with a combination of intellectual clarity and heart. Both reiterated forcefully that loving your brother was the most important thing in life.

The faith they gave me was a blessing when Larry's condition took a turn for the worse and his powers of speech began to fail. I'd feed him breakfast; nurses hovered over him around the clock; doctors kept sticking needles in his arm; the barrage of X-rays continued.

Medicines were just making him worse; he vomited constantly. And they were now feeding him through his stomach.

At one point, my brother was in such excruciating pain that I demanded the doctors give him a morphine injection. One doctor started screaming at me, saying it wasn't warranted. I lost my temper and screamed back, and the two of us nearly came to blows. Finally the injection was administered, and Larry's agony subsided.

Ceil was frightened that this daily confrontation with death would shatter me and bring back my agoraphobia. Phobics have a desperately difficult time facing the reality of needles, pins, blood tests and urine tests.

I could understand her fear, but things were different now. I had Jesus. I was covered by the umbrella of his love. I knew he was watching over me and giving me strength.

I also knew that he loved Larry, and I wanted Larry to know it too.

This was delicate ground. My brother's initial resistance to the idea of Christ had been powerful. Later, seeing my transformation and the inner healing that had taken place in my soul, he had softened somewhat, even to remarking, 'Well. . . at least all this Christian stuff does you some good. . . but it's not for me.'

The last thing I wanted to do was pressurise him into accepting a spiritual idea that he didn't genuinely feel. When he asked me to pray for him, I deliberately kept the words neutral, making no specific references.

At these times, I would hold his hand and occasionally—when he could muster up the effort—he squeezed my fingers.

He lost more and more weight—3½ st in eight weeks. I

willed myself not to concentrate on his gaunt, skeletal frame, but only to think of the brother I had known before.

When he was close to the end, he whispered, 'Do you think I'll lose my job?' Hearing that, the full force of my grief washed over me.

It was Larry's last night. I couldn't sleep, and I'm eternally grateful now that I stayed awake. At three in the morning, I heard my brother's voice—a parched, strangled, almost inaudible sound.

He seemed to be asking a question, but I couldn't make out what it was.

'Tell me, Larry,' I said. 'I'm here. What do you want?'

'Am I dying, Al?'

'No one dies,' I said. 'Not as long as they have Jesus.'

'Can I have. . . can I accept. . . ?' He couldn't finish the sentence.

'He's right here with you,' I said.

'I'm scared.'

'There's no need to be scared,' I said, 'because he's here.'

'What do I have to do?' my brother mumbled. 'I want him with me.'

My brother—of his own free will, without any prompting from Ceil or me—had accepted Jesus. I felt stunned at his unexpected surrender, as well as overwhelming relief. Now he would be cherished and protected.

Larry passed away at 12.31pm the next day, on Yom Kippur, leaving this earth to go forward on the second lap of his journey.

The producer part of my brother would have been satisfied by his funeral.

I had rarely been in the direct centre of my brother's life, so it hadn't dawned on me how deeply loved he was. The chapel was packed, like a theatre on opening night, about to burst from over-crowding. It seemed as if everyone on the Lorimar set—where he had produced *Knots Land-*

*ing*—was there. Donna Summer sat with Ceil and Dana, who was inconsolable at the loss of her uncle.

In keeping with Larry's request that his funeral be upbeat, I taped music from all his shows and played it in the background. 'I've never been morbid during my lifetime,' he once said to me. 'And I don't want to be morbid when I die.'

We all tried to maintain the positive tone Larry wanted. Michele Lee, who had worked with Larry on the musical *Seesaw*, as well as *Knots Landing*, gave a beautiful speech that emphasised his charm and humour. David Jacobs, creator of *Knots Landing*, pointed out how disciplined he was, what comically extreme care he took with his notes and papers.

And co-producer Michael Filerman paid him the ultimate tribute when he said, 'Larry taught me about courage. He taught me to be myself, and not to be ashamed, and I'll always be grateful.'

When I gave the eulogy, I made an effort to match the light, breezy attitudes surrounding me. This pretence lasted for less than a minute; all at once, I broke down completely. Never had I experienced such a wrenching, total loss of control.

I thought of my brother, of his gifts, his talent, his intelligence and wit. I thought of the lost years, the years we could have shared if misunderstandings, false pride and foolish prejudice hadn't blocked our way. Somehow, if we had both tried a little harder to push past the destructive interference of our parents, we might have been reconciled sooner.

I asked myself why it had taken death to bring about a closeness that could have so joyously enriched our lives.

This kind of conjecture was useless. It was more important to concentrate on what we *had* accomplished. In those final weeks, we had dropped the artificial facades and become, at last, brothers in every sense: brothers as friends, brothers as colleagues and brothers in spirit.

On the way back to my seat, I was surprised to see Darryl. We embraced wordlessly.

'I loved him,' Darryl said. 'Do you think he knew that?'

'He knew it,' I told him, and I was able to say, without envy, without reservation, 'You were the person he loved more than anyone else in the world.'

# 17

## *The Morning After*

There's got to be a morning after
If we can hold on through the night
We have a chance to find the sunshine
Let's keep on looking for the light

It was 1994, and I could look back over the past with a sense of unclouded joy. I had survived. Elvis Presley, Jimi Hendrix, Jackie Wilson, Janis Joplin, Mama Cass, Keith Moon and scores of others were dead of self-imposed excess, but I had come through, and so had all the members of my Brill Building generation. Collectively, we had cut through the scarring underbrush and emerged intact. Burt Bacharach had won another Oscar. Carole King established herself as a magnificent actress in Broadway's *Bloodbrothers*, and Mann and Weil were still turning out hits together.

I was proud of my generation. They had changed with the times. All of us had been willing to keep pace with trends, not lock ourselves in. Our early training—that Don Kirshner insistence on writing for 'the date' no matter what kind of artist—had given us the flexibility to switch gears at a moment's notice.

We had all chosen to live and grow; to keep trying, rather than be destroyed when the winds turned against us.

Joel got himself into physical shape again, slimming down to his proper weight. Shortly afterwards he fell in love and remarried. His wife, Jennifer Carter, hailed worldwide for being the first woman to dive down to the Titanic in a submersible, shares his interest in films and music. But their strongest bond is a willingness to grant each other freedom. They know, from past experience, how harmful it can be when a relationship becomes a struggle for control. They are friends, team mates; and the laughter and warmth they radiate is wonderful to witness.

Life, I've discovered, can be as open and free, as packed with possibilities, as the shiny, heaven-lit road described in the Bible, or as dark and closed as the wardrobe that once imprisoned me as a child. All of us have to choose. My mother and father, unlike my Brill Building friends, chose the darkness. I compromised, putting my head out of doors, 'looking for the light', while my feet remained firmly planted inside.

I couldn't stay behind or pull free, and the emotional split produced confusion and rage. Rage I couldn't deal with constructively because I couldn't admit I had it. My mother's 'be nice' kept the anger buried and permitted it to grow.

I've tried all my life to be gentle and softly-spoken, but everyone has natural anger. Things disturb and hurt us, and a certain amount of healthy hostility is needed to defend ourselves in a crisis. If someone tries to kill us, we're simply handing him the knife if we behave with inappropriate niceness.

My agoraphobia was repressed anger. Growing up I felt rage because my needs were never met. I resented being an adult from the cradle on, while my father stayed a child. I resented being a responsible working 'man' when my friends were still concerned about baseball games and summer camp.

Later on, I resented the role of 'parent' to everyone, even though I elected to take that role on. I wanted someone to say, 'Don't worry, I'll take over,' but when Ceil tried to do just that, I fought against her help.

It's hard to ask for assistance; for a personality like mine, it was impossible. Asking for help meant: I'm weak, I can't handle things myself. I'm a failure. And there's always that fear—basic to a person who never had anyone to lean on—that the request for help, once finally made, will be denied; that people will turn their backs on you.

And they well might. This fundamental fear is not without a certain amount of validity. By and large, human beings will extend a hand; but the risk of rejection is there.

*Rejection*—that terrifying word. All frightened people dread it and equate it with emotional death. A friend turns away. A lover wants to end a relationship. A parent is too preoccupied to listen to your problems.

As a person who has fought and survived the rejections of show business, I can say that rejection is largely a matter of what we perceive in advance. When someone—a publisher, a producer—says 'no', you swallow hard, stand up straight and go on. The anticipation of it is often what overwhelms you.

The word 'rejection' is often the word of a victim. It implies 'poor me, I'm unloved'. But critics can strengthen character. If you don't fold up and become defensive, you can learn from them. If being loved and approved of isn't your only focus, you can gain knowledge on how to improve as artist and human being.

It's hard, though I try to do it more and more. Anger can erupt in the face of disapproval and the anger can't be shoved under the rug and ignored. Emotion must be allowed to bubble to the surface; and when it does, it can be dealt with. Handled and resolved by prayer and by faith.

Faith, I've learned, calms a troubled spirit, helps people *hear* what's going on in their minds and hearts. Prayer reduces the static. Any prayer, contrary to the belief of those who must always be in control, doesn't imply weakness. It only admits a willingness to trust in something higher than yourself; to admit there *is* something higher.

The miracle I experienced after discovering Jesus Christ was a new ability to listen and truly hear a playback of myself. It's difficult to figure out what you want when you're totally outer-directed, when your only objective is satisfying others. You never stop to ask: 'Is this what I need? Is it good for me? Is it constructive?' Only: 'I'll show them. I'll prove myself.'

But if you put yourself in the hands of a higher power, if you allow love to come in, the noises diminish and you truly begin to know yourself.

Wholehearted acceptance of Jesus, for me, is the miracle cure that packs more potency than any doctor's prescription. I had read so many self-help books, but I found that the Bible is the greatest self-help book of them all.

I've heard people say—as Larry once did—that Christianity makes people less tolerant, more judgemental. It's exactly the opposite. People frequently use, and twist, Jesus' words, but in truth, Jesus stressed one thing—love. Never judgement, only that you love your fellow man. In my confusion and sense of rejection, I had judged Larry, and in the end I was able to love him as a brother without being critical of his choices or his lifestyle. It only pains me that he made decisions which cost him his life and prematurely robbed Dana, Ceil and me of the joy of his presence.

All of us, having witnessed first hand the indescribable agonies Larry suffered, are determined to do what we can to prevent others from experiencing such pain. We've become deeply involved in the battle against AIDS and cancer, particularly as it affects children, calling out at every turn for compassion and love. Raising money through our two foundations has become our number one priority.

We continually find the strength to do this through Jesus, reminding ourselves of the scripture, 'I can do all things through him who strengthens me.'

Loving and worshipping Jesus offers a wonderful unexpected bonus: a deeply personal relationship with a *friend*—not someone formidable and forbidding.

Having Jesus in my life helped me to think in positive terms. With practice it becomes easier to concentrate on beauty—the trusting hand of a child, the sweep of a calm blue ocean—than to dwell on negative, self-defeating images.

I drifted naturally towards people who genuinely cared and wanted the best for me. I avoided those who criticised me 'for my own good', or attempted to manipulate me for their own selfish gain.

My sense of wholeness was restored. I no longer had to play the convoluted phobic game; the game that said: people will feel sorry for me if I have agoraphobia, and then they'll take notice and forgive me for not living up to their expectations.

I surrendered all attempts at control, reminding myself, 'We do the possible; God does the impossible.'

And through him I had, after all, accomplished things I once felt *were* impossible. I had overcome agoraphobia by trusting him. I had been able to forgive my mother once I surrendered my angers and put myself in his hands.

And I had been able to excavate the love for my brother, so long buried in my heart.

None of it would have been possible without deciding to lead a God-centred rather than world-centred life. I felt I belonged to Jesus; I found my self-esteem through him and continued to gain confidence through his words and Spirit.

I realise now that we're all rats in a maze, chasing around the same corridors to resolve old wounds, never pausing to evaluate new alternatives. Jess Moody once said, 'Insanity is doing the same thing over again, expecting different results.' Larry and I were going to make our parents acknowledge what we were doing. If we'd taken the time to look at them, *really* look, we'd have understood that they were rats in a maze, unthinkingly reacting to unresolved conflicts of their own. They were children too.

We'd have understood, at last, that a child isn't capable of raising another child.

I find great satisfaction these days in writing songs for the Christian market. England's pop sensation of the 1960s, Helen Shapiro, is now a dedicated believer and has sung our spiritual songs. I'm grateful to her, as well as Irene Cara, Marilyn McCoo, Frankie Valli and Tony Orlando for conveying my beliefs so beautifully.

Joel and I also focus extensively on family-orientated ventures, particularly animation. There's nothing more satisfying than the light in a child's eyes when he's enjoying animated stories, and that glow from a young boy or girl is the inspiration for specials we've done such as *The Magic Paintbrush, The Original Top Ten* (a musical version of the Ten Commandments), *Precious Moments* and *Charles Dickens' David Copperfield*, a primetime animated musical which we adapted for television and which I co-produced. We also wrote the theme song for a now-classic feature film *All Dogs Go to Heaven*.

Many stars felt as we did, and were excited to lend their voices and talents to our family projects, among them Julian Lennon, Sheena Easton, Freddie Jackson, James Ingram, Melissa Manchester, Kelly Le Brock and that great British actor Michael York.

I still work diligently; I always will. The pressures of Hollywood continue to be intense, especially since I've done a great deal of film and stage producing in recent years. But I can handle them because I have the blessing of God's grace, a rock-solid spirituality, and the support of treasured friends in the industry who share my vision. I have a role model and clearly marked guidelines I never found at home. Most of all, I've discovered a faith that has helped me escape the darkness and find my own morning after.

# Appendix
## Faith over Fear

*1. Deal with your emotions honestly*

(a) Allow genuine emotion to surface. Don't repress it or be ashamed of it.

(b) Admit you have the phobia. Admit your feelings of guilt and loneliness.

(c) Forgive yourself and those who have hurt you. Forgiveness makes true love possible.

(d) Don't accept the guilt others place on you. Learn to laugh at it.

(e) Forget the past and live in the present. In order to forgive we must learn to forget. Don't forgive with words and cling to old wounds.

*2. Change any physical habits that affect you emotionally, spiritually and mentally*

(a) Avoid thinking of drugs as a cure-all. At best, they offer a temporary relief.

(b) Learn to enjoy life by being with positive people.

(c) Get the advice of a doctor. Go for a physical check-up to make sure you're not having a heart attack or suffering from some other physically caused condition.

(d) Be careful what you eat and drink. Caffeine and sodium are not good for the system or for the blood pressure – especially for phobics, who are so highly sensitised.

*3. Take control of your mind and thoughts. Guard your heart and guard your emotions; don't let them get trapped*

(a) Direct your mind to dwell on present, positive things. Close your eyes, in the morning or at night, and visualise beautiful scenes. Think about the sea, the majestic mountains. Think about people you admire. Above all, think of God's love.

(b) Visualise yourself letting your fears go. Meditate. Picture the fears actually leaving your body. Watch them go one by one.

(c) Trust God to take control.

(d) Refresh your mind with things you enjoy. Listen to comedy tapes or sweet, soothing music.

4. *Make a note of the people you spend time with – avoid spending time with those who pull you down, and spend more with those who build you up*

(a) Learn to say three phrases: 'It's OK', 'I'm sorry', and 'I understand'. This goes for the phobic helper as well as the phobic himself.

(b) Learn to put your loved ones first.

5. *Every minute you stay firm is more ammunition against panic. Stand firm when the fears return and continue to trust in God*

# Discography

## Al Kasha

*Irresistible You*
  Bobby Darin
  Billy J. Kramer
  Bobby Peterson

*I'm Comin' on Back to You*
*My Empty Arms*
*Sing (and tell the blues so long)*
*Lonely Life*
*Forever and a Day*
*Each Night I Dream of You*
*The River*
  Jackie Wilson

*Where There's a Will There's a Way*
*Sing (and tell the blues so long)*
*One of Them*
*No Matter What I Do*
*Teardrops Are Falling*
  Al Kasha

*At Night*
  Neil Diamond

*Sing (and tell the blues so long)*
  Johnny O'Keefe

*Don't Come Crying to Me*
  Roy Hamilton

*Operation Heartbreak*
  Aretha Franklin

*The Dancing Man*
  Cab Calloway

*The Switcheroo*
  Hank Ballard

*One Is a Lonely Number*
*Someone Mentioned Your Name*
  Adam Wade

*Never Again*
  Dinah Washington
  Erma Franklin

*It's Over*
  Erma Franklin

*Big Italian Moon*
*Gegetta*
  James Darren

*Moonlight Promises*
  Petula Clark

*Kisses*
*All of Us*
  Johnny Nash

*Everlasting*
  Four Evers

*Lonely Summer*
  The Four Tops

*Here Comes the Pain*
*My Reputation*
  Johnny Restivo

*Just a Little Line*
  Buzz Clifford

*Judy's Not There*
  The Yogi Three

*Brokenhearted*
*Lord I Give You Praise*
  Brush Arbor

*Who Killed Teddy Bear*
  Leslie Uggams

*I Don't Wanna Go On*
*Benefit of the Doubt*
  Vi Velasco

## Al Kasha and
## Joel Hirschhorn

*The Morning After*—Oscar winner:
Best Song, 1973
*We May Never Love Like This Again*—
Oscar winner: Best Song, 1975
*In Too Deep*
*Make Tomorrow's Memories Now*
*Paper Bridges*
  Maureen McGovern

*Candle on the Water*—Oscar nominees: Best Song, 1977
  Helen Reddy

*I'd Like to Be You for a Day*—
Golden Globe nominee: Best
Song, 1976
  Donny Osmond

*Don't Wake Me Up in the Morning,*
*Michael*
  The Peppermint Rainbow
  Carolyn Franklin

*Let's Start All Over Again*
*One More Mountain to Climb*
  Ronnie Dove

*Your Time Hasn't Come Yet, Baby*
  Elvis Presley

*The Old Fashioned Way*
*Like Roses*

*Little Fool, I Love You*
*Take Me Away*
*I Have Lived*
*Turn Out the Lights*
  Charles Aznavour

*The Old Fashioned Way*
  Fred Astaire
  Shirley Bassey
  Jack Jones
  Peters and Lee
  Helen Reddy
  George Burns and over
    200 other artists

*No One But You*
*Love Survives* (duet with Freddie
Jackson)
  Irene Cara

*Now Are Things in California*
*Roadblock*
*How I Have Everything*
  Nancy Sinatra

*Why Can't You Bring Me Home*
  Jay and the Americans

*He's All You Need*
  Tony Orlando

*Glad That You Were Born*
  Debby Boone

*Everybody Has a Purpose*
  Carman

*Is There a Way Back to Your Arms*
  Anthony Newley

*Ten Below*
  Peter Allen

*Stay and Love Me All Summer*
  Brian Hyland

*Wake Up*
  The Chambers Brothers

*For a Friend*
  The Bugaloos

*My Kind of Lady*
*Dream Chasers*
  The Burrito Brothers

*Charlie I Love Your Wife*
*There's No Sun on Sunset Boulevard*
  Tommy Roe

*I Stand Accused (Of Loving You)*
*Give Me My Freedom*
*Security*
  The Glories

*Two Kinds of Lovers*
  The Fugue Four

*Cloudy*
  The Chicago Loop

*Heaven in My Arms*
  The Whitneys

*You Never Told Me About Goodbye*
  Susie Allanson

*I'm Going Back to New York City*
  The Peppermint
    Trolley Company

*I Love You too Much to Lose You*
  Al Martino

*Give Your Woman What She Wants*
  Taj Mahal

*One More Mountain to Climb*
  Solomon King

*With You Girl*
  The Arbors

*Everything Begins With You*
  Debbie Brewer

*Jaywalking*
*Mr. Sebastian*
  The Distant Cousins

*The Brightest Star*
  James Ingram

  Melissa Manchester

*I Wonder*
  Steve Elliott

*Water on Stone*
*Is There Anyone*
  Helen Shapiro

*The Morning After*
  Roy Orbison
  Liberace
  Ferrante and Teicher
  Roger Williams

*It Scares Me*
*Let Tonight Linger On*
  Nancy Ames

*How Good It Used to Be*
  Charlie Rich

*A Time Like This Again*
  Carl Anderson

*I Won't Let You See Me Cry*
  Trini Lopez

*Bad*
  Lesley Gore

*Nova Scotia Lady*
  Bobby Arvon

*Curiosity*
  Moses Tyson

*Souvenir*
  Lovelines

*Someone I Touched*
  Cloris Leachman

*The Song's in Me*
  Bert Sommers

*Anytime You Want Me Just Whistle*
*Silently*
  Bobbi Norris

*Joined at the Heart*
  David Hasselhoff

*Night After Night*
  Tony Christie

*Sleeping Between Two People*
  Vicki Carr

*Showtime for Everyone*
  Sammy Davis Jr.

*The Night Before*
  Mama Cass Elliott

*You Can Count on Beer*
  David Allan Coe/
    Lacey J. Dalton

*Rolling Stone*
  Henry Fonda/James Stewart
    (duet)

*All About Love*
  Clyde McPhatter
*Lies*
  Frankie Valli

*Now I Have Everything*
  Gary Morris

*Don't Let Me Catch You in His
  Arms*
  The Razor's Edge

*I'd Love to Give My Love Away*
  The Exiles

*The Subject Was Roses*
  Buddy Greco

*Let's Pretend*
*It Happened So Long Ago*
  Ron Murphy

*Look Again*
  The Brooklyn Bridge

*I'm Taking You With Me*
  Tommy Leonetti

*All God's Children*
  Marilyn McCoo

*You Better Know*
  Patti Austen

*My Name Is Alice*
  Marie Osmond

*The Rivermen*
  Johnny Rodriguez

*Living Is Dying Without You*
  Peggy Lee

*To the Top*
  Nell Carter

*I'll Be Your Hero*
  Julian Lennon

*Is There Anyone*
  Sheena Easton

*All Kinds of People*
  Phyllis McGuire

*Don't Make Me a Memory*
  Jesse Lopez

**Soundtracks**

*Seven Brides for Seven Brothers*
  Tony nominee: Best Score, 1983
*Pete's Dragon*
  Oscar nominee: Best Song
    Score, 1977
*The Towering Inferno*
  Oscar winner: Best Song, 1975
*The Poseidon Adventure*
  Oscar winner: Best Song, 1973
*Speedway*
*The April Fools*
*Donny and Marie—Songs from
    Their TV show*
*The Grasshopper*
*The Original Top Ten*
  Angel Award Winner: Best
    Score, 1990
*Lovelines*
*David Copperfield*
*Take This Job and Shove It*
*Gidget Goes to Rome*
*A Precious Moments Christmas*

# Acknowledgements

Aaron Meza
Aaron Schroeder
Actor's Equity
    Association
Adam Wade
AFTRA
Ahmet Ertegun
Al Gallico
Al Nevins
Al Ruddy
Al Schlesinger
Al Schwartz
Al Waller
Alan Thomas
Albert Spevak
Alvin Goldfine
Amanda Sudano
Amfar
Andrea Martin
Andy Rigrod
Andy Williams
Angela Lansbury
Anna Martinez-Holler
Anna-Sue Greenberg
Anthony Newley
APLA
Archie Jordan
Aretha Franklin
Arlene Ludwig
Army & Selma

Archerd
Arnold Stiefel
Arthur Allan
    Seidelman
Arthur Hamilton
Arthur Jacobs
Artie Butler
Artie Mogull
Artie Ripp
ASCAP
Barbara Cane
Barbara Fanto
Barbra Streisand
Barney Ales
Barry Josephson
Barry Kroft
Barry Reardon
Barry White
Bee Gees
Ben Scotti
Bernice & George
    Altschul
Berry Gordy, Jr.
Bertha & Tamala
    Joffrion
Betty Comden
Bill Bennett
Bill Immerman
Bill Mechanic
Bill Sheppard

Billboard Magazine
Billy Goldenberg
Billy J. Kramer
Blossom Kahn
BMI
Bob Angelotti
Bob Austin
Bob Banner
Bob Crewe
Bob Esposito
Bob Gaudio
Bob Halley
Bob King
Bob Rehme
Bob Shea
Bobby Arvon
Bobby Darin
Bobby Peterson
Brian Hyland
Brian Rohan
Brooklyn Sudano
Brooks & Marilyn
    Arthur
Bruce Lundvall
Bruce Sudano
Bud Paxson
Buddy Greco
Burt Bacharach
Cal Scaglione
Cal Thomas

217

Candy Parton
Cardon Walker
Carly Simon
Carol Bayer-Sager
Carol Curb
Carol Ostroff
Carolyn Franklin
Casey Kasem
Charles Aznavour
Charles Calello
Charles Koppelman
Charles Lisanby
Charles Monk
Charles Morgan
Charles Nelson Reilly
Charlie Rich
Cher
Chicago Loop
Chip Murray
Chita Rivera
Chris Montan
Christian Slater
Chuck Berry
Chuck Fries
Chuck Kaye
Chuck Tilley
Clark Mathias
Clive Davis
Clyde McPhatter
Coleman & Carel
  Luck
Congressman Joel
  Wachs
Connie Stevens
Constance McCashin
Constance Towers
Creative Artists
  Agency
Curtis Williams
Cy Coleman
Daily Variety
Dan Lyon

Danny Bond
Danny & Julie
  Bramson
Dara Bernard Evans
Dave Rubinson
David Allan Coe
David Braun
David Garland
David Geffen
David Grahame
David Hasselhoff
David Jacobs
David Kapralik
David Landay
David Picker
David Waters
Debbie Reynolds
Debby Boone
Della Reese
Dennis C. Stanfill
Derek Prince
Derek Wilson
Dianne Bennett
Dick Berg
Dick Clark
Dick Rolfe
Dinah Shore
Dinah Washington
Dom DeLuise
Don Bluth
Don Costa
Donald Kushner
Don Mathison
Donna Mills
Donna Summer
Donnie Rubin
Donny Osmond
Donny Rubin
Dorothy Miller
Doug Frank
Dr Billy Graham
Dr. Jess Moody

Dr. Robert Schuller
Dwayne Ward
Dyson Lovell
E.Y. (YIP) Harburg
Earle Hagen
Ed Cramer
Ed Lubin
Ed Matthews
Ed Silvers
Eleanor Levy
Elvis Presley
Emile Petrone
Eric Greenspan, Esq.
Erma Bombeck
Erma Franklin
Ernest & Tova
  Borgnine
Ernie K. Doe
Etta James
Eydie Gorme
Florence Greenberg
Floyd Cramer
Frances Preston
Frank & Bunny
  Wilson
Frank Capra, Jr.
Frank Military
Frank Paris
Frank Sinatra
Frank Wilson
Frankie Valli
Fred Astaire
Fred Ebb
Fred Rappaport
Freddie & The
  Dreamers
Freddie Bienstock
Freddie Jackson
Gabriel Ferrer
Garry Marshall
Gary Collins
Gary Earl

Gary Krisel
Gary LeMel
Gary Morris
Gene and Harry
  Goodman
Gene Kelly
Gene Saks
George Alpert
George Burns
George David Weiss
George Garvarentz
George Goldner
George Jensen
George Pincus
Georges Meyerstein
Gerry Robinson
Gigi Gerard
Gina Delgado
Glodean White
Gloria Loring
Goddard Leiberson
Gordon Stulberg
Governor Pete Wilson
Greg Sill
Greg Smith
Gregory Peck
Hal David
Hal Prince
Hank & Linda
  Marmor
Hank Ballard
Hank Hunter
Happy Goday
Harland Goodman
Harold & Edie
  Greenberg
Harold Kleiner
Harold Wald
Harry Archinal
Haskell Wexler
Helen Reddy
Helen Shapiro

Henry Fonda
Henry Mancini
Herb Eiseman
Howard Fast
Howard Greenfield
Howard Keel
Howie Mandel
International Creative
  Management
Ira Howard
Irene Cara
Irv Levin
Irving Ludwig
Irving Mansfield
Irwin & Jackie Mazur
Irwin Allen
Irwin Kostal
Irwin Pincus
Irwin Robinson
Irwin Schuster
It's A Beautiful Day
Ivan Mogull
Jack Jones
Jackie Wilson
Jacqueline Susann
James Ingram
James Taylor
Jane Powell
Jay & The Americans
Jay Kenoff
Jay Morgenstern
Jeff Barry
Jeff Holder
Jeff Parsons
Jeff Wald
Jeffrey Katzenberg
Jennie Trias
Jennifer Warnes
Jerome Robbins
Jerry Belson
Jerry Courtland
Jerry Fielding

Jerry Goldsmith
Jerry Herman
Jerry Isenberg
Jerry Weintraub
Jerry Wexler
Jesse Lopez
Jim Buick
Jim Collier
Jim Fitzgerald
Jim Miller
Jimmy Brochu
Jimmy Clanton
Jimmy Nederlander
Jimmy Stewart
Joan Rivers
Jodi Benson
Joe Green
Joe Kolsky
Joe Mazucca
Joe Smith
Joel Greenberg
Joel Roman
Joel Sill
Joey Gmerek
John Cacavas
John David Kalodner
John Gavin
John Kander
John Miller
John Newman
John Pacalubo
John Rainbow
John Ritter
John Williams
Johnny Cash
Johnny Grant
Johnny Mercer
Johnny Nash
Johnny Rodriguez
Johnny Tillotson
Jon Butcher
Jon Crawley

Jonathan Stone
Joseph Marcel
Joyce Bogart-Trabulus
Jule Styne
Julian Lennon
Julie Horton
Julie Lipsius
Karen Huybrechts
Karen Rodriguez
Karen Swallow
Kathie Lee Gifford
Kathy Reesemyer
Kelly LeBrock
Ken Anderson
Ken Hertz
Ken Yates
Kenny Kommisar
Kevin Dobson
Kimberly Coy
King Curtis
Lacy J. Dalton
Lalo Schiffrin
Lamont Dozier
Larry Kusik
Larry Lee
Larry Poland
Lauren Bacall
Laythan Armour
Lee Phillips, Esq.
Lee Zhito
Leon Brettler
Lesley Gore
Leslie Shapiro
Leslie Uggams
Lester Sill
Liberace
Linda Ehrlich
Linda Hopkins
Linda Mancuso
Linda Perry
Lionel Newman
Lisa Brown

Lisa Henson
Liza Minnelli
Lonnie Sill
Lord Bernard Delfont
Loretta Munoz
Lou Mitchell
Lou Sudano
Lucille Ball
Luther Dixon
Mack David
Madge Sudano
Malcolm Stewart
Mama Cass Elliott
Margie-Girl Jenkins
Marie Canales
Marilyn & Alan
    Bergman
Marilyn Mark Petrone
Marilyn McCoo
Marilyn McCoo &
    Billy Davis, Jr.
Marion Dougherty
Marion Evans
Mark Ferness
Mark Koren
Martin Berger
Martin Gould
Marty Ehrlichman
Marty Ostrow
Marvin Cane
Marvin Hamlisch
Marvin Krauss
Mary & Andrew
    Gaines
Mary Ann Mobley
Mary Catherine
    Harold
Mary Dorr
Mary Elizabeth Mas-
    trantonio
Mary Ellen & Gerardo
    Bernard

Maurice White
Mel Bly
Melissa Manchester
Merrill Dean
Michael Filerman
Michael Barnathan
Michael Bennett
Michael Eisner
Michael Jackson
Michael Kerker
Michael Lloyd
Michael Nadel
Michael York
Michele Lee
Mike Curb
Mike Medavoy
Mike Nichols
Mike Stewart
Milt Goldstein
Mimi Sommer
Mitchel Ryder
Molly Young
Mort Lachman
Moses Tyson
Mr & Mrs. Galo
    Medina
Music Theatre
    International
Nancy Ames
Nancy DeMoss
Nancy DeMoss, Jr.
Nancy Knutsen
Nancy Sinatra
NARAS
National Academy of
    Songwriters
Ned Shankman
Neil Anderson
Neil Bogart
Neil Diamond
Neil Simon
Nell Carter

Nelson Riddle
Nesuhi Ertegun
Nick Alphin
Norm Prescott
Norman and Gayle
  Sedawie
Norman Brokaw
Norman Singer
Norman Weiser
Oliver Witherspoon
Onna White
Pam Howar
Pam Hyatt
Pastor Brent Price
Pastor Fred Price
Pastor Jack Hayford
Pastor Phillip & Holly
  Wagner
Pat Robertson
Pat Tourk Lee
Patti Austin
Paul Adler
Paul and Jan Crouch
Paul Anka
Paul Baratta
Paul Blake
Paul Leka
Paul Sherman
Paul Williams
Paula Perry
Peggy Lee
Peppermint Rainbow
Peppermint Trolley
  Co.
Peter Allen
Peter Engel
Peter Guber
Peter Locke
Peter Nero
Peters & Lee
Petula Clark
Phil Steinberg

Phyllis Diller
Piz Zadora
Plant Life
President Jimmy
  Carter and Roslyn
  Carter
President Ronald
  Reagan & Nancy
  Reagan
Rabbi David Baron
Ralph Ehrenpreis
Randy Hart
Randy Phillips
Ray Conniff
Ray Golden
Ray Ruff
Ray Stark
Ray Stevens
Raymond & Babette
  Scully
Raymond Wagner
Red & Alycia Buttons
Regis Philbin
Rev. Derek Prince
Rhoda Bressler
Rich Wiseman
Richard & Carol
  Herschenfeld
Richard Fischoff
Richard Graff
Richard Ingber
Richard Perry
Richard Rodgers
Richard Schulenberg
Rick Reinert
Rick Smith
Rick Unger
Ritchie Adams
Robby Benson
Robert Guillaime
Robert John
Robert Kraft

Robert Light
Robert Osborne
Rodney Dangerfield
Roger Gordon
Roger Williams
Ron Anton
Ron Dante
Rona Barrett
Ronnie Dove
Roy Acuff
Roy Disney, Jr.
Roy Orbison
Roy Hamilton
Russ Regan
Sal Chiantia
Sal Ianucci
Sally Berg
Sam Butcher
Sam Goldwyn, Jr.
Sam Haskell
Sammy Cahn
Sammy Davis, Jr.
Sandy Gallin
Sandy Krinski
Scott Baio
Scott 'Frosti' Simpson
Screen Actors Guild
Senator Dianne
  Feinstein
Sheena Easton
Sheila Witkin
Shelley Winters
Sherry Lansing
Shirley Bassey
Shirley Maclaine
Sid Ganis
Sid Wyche
Snuff Garrett
Sonny Bono
Spence Berland
Squire Rushnell
Stan Freeman

Stan Moress
Stan Seiden
Stanley Catron
Stanley Mills
Stanley Silverberg
Stephanie Edwards
Stephen Greenberg
Stephen Sondheim
Steve Lawrence
Steve Schaclin
Steve Steinberg
Steve Stone
Steven Seagal
Stevie Wonder
Stuart Berton
Sue Mengers
Sue Wolfe
Susie Allanson
Taj Mahal
Talia Shire
Tanya Tucker
Ted Baehr
Ted Danz
Terry Semel
The Academy of
    Motion Picture Arts
    & Sciences
The American Theatre
    Wing
The Arbors
The Bklyn. Bridge
The Brokaw Company
The Bugaloos
The Burrito Bros.
The Chambers Bros.
The Country Music
    Association
The Directors Guild
The Exiles
The Four Evers
The Four Seasons
The Four Tops

The Glories
The Gospel Music
    Association
The Hardy Boys
The Hollywood
    Reporter
The Lettermen
The Light Agency
The Osmonds
The Razor's Edge
The Songwriters
    Guild
The Ventures
The Whitneys
The Wild Ones
The William Morris
    Agency
The Writers Guild
Thea Zavin
Theron Raines
Tim O'Brien
Tim Penland
Tim Robertson
Tino Barzie
Tobin Matthews
Todd Brabec
Todd Leavitt
Tom Bahler
Tom Catalano
Tom Lloyd
Tommy Culla
Tommy Leonetti
Tommy Mottola
Tommy Tune
Tony Christie
Tony Scotti
Tony Smith
Trini Lopez
Upio Minucci
Valerie Harper
Vice-President Al
    Gore & Tipper Gore

Vice-President Dan
    Quayle & Marilyn
    Quayle
Vicki Carr
Walter Dean
Walter Scharf
Walter Yetnikoff
Wayne Allwine
Wayne Newton
Wendy Sukman
Wes Farrell
William Devane
Willie Dixon
Woody Allen
Yale Wexler
Yvonne De Carlo